POWER
ECONOMICS

POWER ECONOMICS

An Executive's Guide
to Energy Efficiency, Conservation,
and Generation Strategies

ELENA CAHILL

WILEY

Published by John Wiley & Sons, Inc., Hoboken, New Jersey.
Published simultaneously in Canada.

For general information on our other products and services or for technical
support, please contact our Customer Care Department within the United States
at (800) 762-2974, outside the United States at (317) 572-3993, or fax (317)
572-4002.

Wiley publishes in a variety of print and electronic formats and by print-on-
demand. Some material included with standard print versions of this book
may not be included in e-books or in print-on-demand. If this book refers to
media such as a CD or DVD that is not included in the version you purchased,
you may download this material at http://booksupport.wiley.com. For more
information about Wiley products, visit www.wiley.com.

Library of Congress Cataloging-in-Publication Data is Available
ISBN 978-1-119-70770-7 (Hardback)
ISBN 978-1-119-70808-7 (ePDF)
ISBN 978-1-119-70807-0 (ePub

Cover image: © Miguel Navarro / Getty Images
Cover design: Wiley

Printed in the United States of America.
SKY10024270_012121

To Christina and Christopher Cahill, my inspiration and good informants in all matters

CONTENTS

ACKNOWLEDGMENTS

*P*ower *Economics* is a book for thoughtful people who want to cut their energy costs and diminish the harmful effects of climate change. I assure you that we can do both.

I have done my best to convey the complexity and urgency of the matter. I hope that you find the book informative and useful. Working together, we can shed many of our wasteful energy habits and begin the task of building a world that is safe, sustainable, and healthy.

For sharing their time and expertise, I thank the following people: Peter Asmus, Brandon Barnes, Ed Boman, James K. Boyce, Kim Cheslak, Angus Duncan, Matthew Goldberg, Rob Kaye, Tim Kelley, Warren Leon, Jason F. McLennan, Will Needham, Nick Nigro, Sandeep Nimmagadda, Bernie Pelletier, Mark Scully, Hugh Seaton, Nathaniel Stinnett, Amy Thompson, Scott Thompson, Chris Ulbrich, Chris Vigilante, and Elisa Wood. Their professional bios are included in a section at the end of the book.

I also thank Steve Diaz, Juan Manuel Avila Hernandez, Jamie Howland, Andreas Koall, Kristilee LaHaye, Cornelia Lévy-Bencheton, Matheus M. Lima, Bruce Maters, Arthur McAdams, Umberto Olivo, Al Peterson, Akshat Rathi, and Jean-Philippe Taillon for providing valuable insight and information.

I also wish to express my deep appreciation to Sheck Cho, Susan Cerra, and Samantha Enders at Wiley. Last, but not least, I extend my sincere thanks to Mike Barlow, who served as my editorial guide on this project. Thank you, Mike!

Minor portions of *Power Economics* are based on content I developed for a previous book, *The Business of Energy*. I have revised, expanded, and updated all of the content to reflect the current state of our endlessly fascinating energy culture.

INTRODUCTION

Climate change and global warming are not fantasies. They are real. They threaten communities, towns, cities, regions, nations, and continents. Even if you don't care about polar bears and penguins, the effects of melting icecaps and shifting ocean currents will transform your life and the lives of the people around you.

In this book, I will offer practical steps and achievable strategies for reducing the destructive impact of climate change and global warming.

A large part of the problem is caused by CO_2 gas released into the atmosphere when we burn fossil fuels to create energy. Yes, we need energy to live and to sustain our economies. But we don't need to burn fossil fuels and release CO_2 gas at levels that will result in a global catastrophe.

There are reasonable alternatives to our current practices. None of the ideas that I describe in this book are entirely new or totally unfamiliar. They aren't extreme or bizarre. They won't require harsh or draconian measures to work. All of them follow basic rules of common sense.

Every idea and process described in this book, if performed reasonably well, will put money in your pocket. You will not only save money, you will probably make money—and you will take important steps toward saving the planet.

Energy efficiency, I would argue, is more of a journey than a battle. It starts with small steps, taken at the local and state levels.

This is a matter of identifying and then practicing good habits in our daily lives, at home and at work.

Yes, it would be nice if the federal government would step up and play a more active role in preserving the environment and preparing for the disastrous effects of climate change. But I'm not waiting for national politicians to rescue us.

I firmly believe that we can mitigate many of the negative impacts of climate change and global warming through community efforts and grassroots campaigns. Please don't wait for a top-down solution. That isn't going to happen. Instead of waiting for someone else to solve our problems, let's figure out how we can work together at the local and state levels to develop practical fixes.

I am confident that if we move forward purposefully, with open eyes and a strong sense of resolve, we will turn the tide. We have the power and the strength to accomplish the mission. And we have a responsibility to future generations. Let's not drop the ball. We can do this!

Quick Basic Concepts

I'm not a scientist or an engineer. In conversations, I tend to use words such as *energy* and *power* interchangeably, yet they have different meanings and it's important to understand the distinction between them.

- **Energy** comes in many forms, such as mechanical, chemical, thermal, electrical, and radioactive. Energy is required to perform work and it's typically measured in joules. Calories are also a measure of energy.

■ **Power** describes how quickly or slowly energy is consumed when it's doing work. Power is typically measured
in watts (W) and kilowatts (kW).

I also speak often about **energy efficiency**, which refers to
the concept of minimizing energy loss during the process of
doing work. When a device or a process is "energy efficient,"
that usually means it's doing the most amount of work with
the least waste.

Now let's switch from physics to economics. I mention
financial incentives several times in this book because they
are fundamental to jump-starting the behavioral changes we
need to solve our energy problems. In the United States,
we've been blessed with an abundance of energy sources.
As a result, we haven't been forced to think much about
using energy efficiently.

We no longer have that luxury. We still have plenty of
energy sources, but it's becoming increasingly clear that our
atmosphere has a limited capacity for absorbing the harmful
by-products of our energy-intensive economy.

If we don't get serious about using energy more efficiently,
we risk losing the world we love. That's why we need to change
our energy habits and use energy more wisely. One of the best
ways to help people change their habits is by providing them
with tangible incentives and rewards for their new behaviors.

Why are incentives necessary? Because it's highly unrealistic to expect large numbers of people to suddenly abandon
their long-standing habits and embrace unfamiliar ones, even
when there are logical and compelling reasons for adopting
new behaviors. We're all creatures of habit, and old habits die hard.

It's also completely unrealistic to expect businesses to adopt energy-saving strategies that won't generate ROI (return on investment) for seven or eight years. Businesses need to see ROI within two years, and that's where incentives can make all the difference. With the right financial incentives, most of the business owners that I know are happy to invest in energy projects.

Well-written rules and regulations can also serve as incentives. People, companies, and governments generally follow rules, especially when those rules are enforced and there are penalties for not following them. The use of coal to generate electricity has fallen sharply in recent years, due in part to regulations that make coal less economical than other fuels. Because the health risks associated with burning coal are inarguable, most people are more than okay with the idea of using less coal. But laws, such as The Clean Air Act and The Clean Water Act, which require industries to reduce pollutants,[1] create the incentives necessary to initiate and sustain meaningful change.

Together, we're all standing at the threshold of a new era, and nobody can say with absolute certainty what will happen next. If it takes some incentives to get the ball rolling in the right direction, I'm all for them.

Ten years from now, we won't need to incentivize people to use energy more carefully and conscientiously. Good energy practices will be considered normal. They will be an invisible part of everyday life. Today, however, we need those incentives to get us across the threshold. They're playing an important role by helping us move forward as a society that cares about the environment and the quality of our lives.

It's a Calling

Similar to many people in the energy business, I am intensely passionate about my work. Here's why: Every time I help my customers reduce wasted energy and save money by using energy more efficiently, I know that I am making the world a better place for future generations. I feel a strong and direct sense of connection between my work and the quality of living that will be experienced by our children, grandchildren, and great-grandchildren. For me, energy is more than a business—it's a calling.

I hope this book will inspire, encourage, and enable you to move forward with an energy-efficiency project at your home, company, school, park, playground, church, synagogue, mosque, temple, ashram, or wherever you gather as a community. Any building, any structure, and any open space can become the site of an energy project that contributes to reducing our collective carbon footprint. There are a lot of different ways to use energy more wisely, and this book will show you how.

What about the Grid?

You've all heard about "the grid," which has become the common term for describing our fantastically complex network for delivering electricity from providers to users. It's not unusual for someone to approach me after I've given a keynote speech or presentation and tell me that we could solve all of our energy problems if we just modernized our national grid. In a sense, that is true, but it's not especially helpful.

There are multiple power transmission grids or "interconnections" in North America. These grids are synchronous, which means they all deliver power at the same frequency: 60 Hz. Because they are synchronous, they can share power and serve as backups when there are overloads.

But there is no single grid covering North America. Strictly speaking, the grid isn't an official entity—the grid is everything that generates, distributes, and consumes electricity. The grid is us—it is inseparable from our modern culture. Everyone who makes, sells, or uses electricity in any way, shape, or form is part of the grid.

So when someone tells me, "We need to reform the grid," it's a lot like hearing someone say, "We need to reform our health-care system." Where do you begin? Do you tear everything down and start from scratch, or do you tinker around the edges and make small improvements wherever you can? How much change is too much and how much is too little? Who is ultimately responsible and who shoulders the costs?

These aren't easy questions. The grid isn't something that arose fully formed after years of rigorous analysis, thorough testing, and meticulous planning. The grid expanded organically, with minimal supervision. For better and for worse, the grid is our offspring. We are its parents and we are ultimately responsible for it.

The grid serves a geographic area of extraordinary size and amazing diversity. Because of its scale and complexity, the grid resists simple solutions. That's one of the reasons we're still burning coal and kerosene to generate electricity in some parts of our nation. Solving the grid's problems might be easier if there were a central authority that could harmonize all of its various pieces. But apart from the Federal Energy Regulatory Commission (FERC), no such overarching authority exists.

Another major obstacle to grid modernization is ignorance. For most of us, the physics of electricity is not a topic of daily conversation. When we think about electricity, we typically imagine it as a substance that moves through wires. But it's not a substance—it's a form of electromagnetic radiation, a wave traveling at nearly the speed of light. Unlike familiar commodities, such as soybeans, corn, eggs, and even crude oil, electricity is consumed moments after it's produced. It's certainly one of the most perishable products we use.

And there are legitimate reasons for relying on multiple sources of energy to produce the continuous flow of electricity we need to sustain our lives and our economies. Inconsistent and variable sources such as wind and solar cannot provide the quantity and quality of electricity required by heavy industry. The same goes for hospitals, data centers, food processing plants, military bases, and other facilities where losing power would be catastrophic.

We cannot simply say to millions of Americans that they won't have any electricity for two or three days because the wind isn't strong enough or the sunshine is blocked by clouds. That's not how our culture works.

I purposely used the word *culture* because I firmly believe that our grid has become synonymous with our culture. When we flip a switch, we expect the lights to go on. When we turn on an air conditioner, we expect the room to get cooler. When we put a grievously ill patient on a ventilator, we expect the ventilator to pump oxygen and to extend the patient's life.

But the costs of variable energy sources are plummeting, making them realistic alternatives to traditional sources such as natural gas and coal. Wind and solar are now eminently viable choices; and with every passing day, the economic argument in their favor grows stronger.

Economics versus Nature

At their primal core, most of our problems with energy arise from an epic and unresolved struggle between temporary human laws and the eternal laws of Mother Nature. If I were placing a long-term bet, I'd put my money on Mother Nature.

Sure, we humans will win a couple of battles, but in the end, Mother Nature will rule. Energy resources follow physical laws. They don't care about the nuances of supply and demand. They don't care about energy trading markets. The molecules, atoms, and electrons that enable us to drive our cars, watch our widescreen TVs, heat our homes in winter, and keep them cool in summer have absolutely no interest in our momentary human desires or in our political systems.

The largest single challenge for power companies is weather. We can't control the weather; all we can do is respond to its changes. The basic advantage of having a collection of grids is that when the weather in one part of the country changes and the demand for power rises or falls, the grids can compensate reasonably quickly, usually within minutes.

Don't Put the Cart before the Horse

When I began writing this book, people asked me why I wasn't focusing more closely on clean energy. My answer is straightforward and simple: you can't put the cart before the horse. You can't do this backwards. Before you can take full advantage of clean energy, you need to be using energy efficiently.

You can have the cleanest energy in the world, but if you're trying to heat or cool a building that is inefficient, you're going to lose money and release more carbon into the air than if you were using your energy efficiently. From my perspective, that's the definition of wasteful. You can have all the good intentions in the world, but if you're wasting energy, you're not helping the planet.

I'm all about making money in ways that are conscientious and socially responsible. I love that some of my friends refer to solar energy as "locally grown, artisanal electrons."

Every process and tactic and trick of the trade that I describe in this book will put cash in your wallet and help the communities around you. That's the beautiful part of becoming energy efficient.

I titled this book *Power Economics* because I deeply believe that if you understand the basic economic principles of energy consumption, you will use energy more wisely and more economically. We've all heard the expression that knowledge is power. Knowing the basics of energy economics will empower you. So let's get started.

Here's an overview of topics I will cover in this book:

Chapter 1: Good Building, Bad Building. Our homes and buildings account for roughly 40 percent of the energy consumed annually in the United States. If our buildings and their systems were optimized to save energy, instead of wasting it, many of our environmental problems would become manageable and ultimately solvable.

Chapter 2: Stabilizing Demand. Your energy costs depend largely on how much energy you use. Yet there is another critical factor in the equation—demand stabilization—and it's incredibly important, both to your checkbook and to our planet's long-term health.

Chapter 3: Why Batteries Matter. Today, most of us are passive consumers of energy produced in large power plants. In the very near future, however, most of us will also become energy producers. The traditional one-to-many model of energy distribution will evolve rapidly into a many-to-many network of users and suppliers. Traditional relationships between energy providers and energy consumers will change radically.

Chapter 4: Energy and the Law. There are federal regulations governing the transmission of energy resources such as natural gas and electricity. But there is no common set of laws or regulations governing how energy is consumed at the individual level. That's left to the states and municipalities. As a result, there's a large degree of variability that makes it difficult to establish coherent energy standards.

Chapter 5: Your Role in Reducing Carbon Output. There is an inescapable link between wealth and carbon output. Bigger is not better, especially from an environmental perspective. If you own a large home, it's probably creating more pollution than your neighbor who owns a small home. The same holds true for automobiles. If you drive a big gas guzzler, you're polluting more than your friend who drives a compact hybrid.

Chapter 6: Focus on What's Doable. Most of the owners and executives I work with are genuinely interested in energy. They like the idea of being smart leaders and good stewards of our shared environment. For them, energy efficiency isn't a passing fad—it's become a deeply embedded part of their lives, influencing every aspect of their worldview. They've become "energy believers."

Chapter 7: The Power of Local Action. "Think globally, act locally" is more than a cliché. We don't like to have solutions imposed on us by largely invisible authorities. We're more likely to adopt homegrown practices that appeal to our innate sense of virtue. In our hearts, most of us are kind and generous. When given the opportunity, I believe that we will act in the common interest and do the right thing.

Chapter 8: Conservation, Efficiency, and Generation. The most direct way of conserving a limited resource is by using less of it. Conservation isn't a new idea; even single-cell organisms such as amoebas and algae have mastered the essentials of conservation. Yet many people resist the simple notion of applying basic conservation techniques to reduce their use of energy. What do microscopic life forms know that we don't?

Chapter 9: Pricing Energy: It's Complicated. The power economy is a complicated beast, shrouded in lore and mystery. In this chapter, we will pull back the curtain and reveal the inner workings of the strangely convoluted ecosystem that supplies power to our homes and businesses. We will also look at some of the main drivers of price fluctuations in energy markets. These drivers include fracking, power plant decommissioning, and the steady rise of renewable energy.

Chapter 10: Understand Your Energy Bills. I cannot overstate the importance of understanding your power bills. In this chapter, we dive deep into the weeds and emerge with a clearer understanding of how you are billed for energy. If you own or operate a business, this knowledge is essential.

Chapter 11: Find the Money. Money is everywhere—but you have to know where to look. Numerous economic incentives are available for conserving energy, using energy more efficiently, and generating energy without harming the environment. This chapter will give you a brief overview of the many financial opportunities that already exist and can be tapped into.

Chapter 12: Educate and Communicate. What good are our beliefs unless we act on them? What's the point of acquiring knowledge if we don't share it? How can we make genuine progress if we talk only with people who already agree with us? In this chapter, we'll take a look at techniques and advice for sharing the message, raising awareness, and dealing with naysayers. Changing the long-standing habits of a culture won't be easy, but I'm confident we can shift the attitudes of enough people to make a lasting difference in how we generate power and consume energy.

As you can see from the topics I've chosen to address, this book is about finding practical answers to genuinely difficult problems that threaten our existence as human beings. I am less interested in theory than I am in achieving practical results. I do not expect to win a Nobel Prize for writing this book, but I do expect that you will glean helpful information that you can begin using immediately to reduce waste, trim your energy costs, formulate doable projects, apply for incentives, complete your projects successfully, and make our world a safer place.

Endnote

1. https://www.eia.gov/energyexplained/coal/coal-and-the -environment.php

Chapter 1

Good Building, Bad Building

Sometimes, the answer to a problem is right in front of your eyes. Conversations about energy often dwell on industries such as transportation, manufacturing, and power generation. Those are worthy targets of our scrutiny. Yet there is a culprit we tend to overlook, perhaps because it is all around us.

Our homes and buildings—referred to as the "built environment"—account for roughly 40 percent of the energy consumed annually in the United States.[1] Residential and commercial structures account for about 70 percent of the electricity we use in a typical year, and are responsible for more than a third of the world's energy-related carbon dioxide (CO_2) emissions.[2] Yet more than two-thirds of the total energy consumed in the United States is wasted, according to data compiled by Lawrence Livermore National Laboratory.[3]

"Most buildings waste energy needlessly, making power plants work harder and putting stress on the electric grid, making energy efficiency in buildings incredibly important," according to the Alliance to Save Energy, a nonprofit, bipartisan alliance of business, government, environmental, and consumer leaders.[4]

I've researched this topic thoroughly and almost every study supports the conclusion that buildings are a vast source of wasted energy. That's why I am adamant about making our buildings more energy efficient. If our buildings and their systems were optimized to save energy, instead of wasting it, many of our environmental problems would become manageable and ultimately solvable.

A growing number of architects and builders are aware of this. Slowly, a consensus is emerging around the need for design and construction strategies that prioritize energy efficiency and reduce waste. The built environment has a permanence that makes it unlike any other human artifact. For better and for worse, the built environment surrounds us. Except for brief periods of time when we're hiking through the woods or sunbathing on a beach, we cannot escape it. Therefore, we need to make it better.

Living Buildings

Jason F. McLennan wishes that buildings were more like flowers. Jason is known as "the Steve Jobs of the green building industry," and he's received the prestigious Buckminster Fuller Prize, the world's top prize for socially responsible design. Jason created the Living Building Challenge,[5] which has been hailed as the most stringent and forward-looking green building program ever developed.

Jason and his firm, McLennan Design,[6] strive to create buildings that are beyond efficient and green. Their goal is designing sturdy, durable buildings that are living parts of their environment, buildings that are more like trees and flowers, drawing energy from natural sources and adding value to the neighborhoods around them.

Living buildings also offer the best long-term economic benefits, according to Jason. "You don't pay energy bills or water bills because the building is producing its own energy and water," he says. Living buildings such as the Bullitt Center, a six-story Class A office building in Seattle, also compost and recycle their own waste materials, eliminating sewer bills and greatly reducing the costs of waste removal. "The goal is creating habitats instead of destroying them," Jason says. "We're not just trying to be 'less bad'—we're pursuing a holistic model that is regenerative for the planet."

Living buildings are constructed from nontoxic materials, making them healthier workspaces. Use of cement, which accounts for 8 percent of the world's CO_2 emissions[7] and is a prime component of concrete, is limited to the building's foundational elements.

"Above the second floor, the Bullitt Center is constructed with heavy timber framing, recalling Seattle's history of heavy timber warehouses. One hundred percent of the wood used is Forest Stewardship Council certified, ensuring it came from a responsibly managed forest, according to the Bullitt Center website. "Using wood sequesters carbon for the life of the building, with 545 metric tons of carbon locked away in the Bullitt Center for the next 250 years."[8]

Jason says he feels energized and optimistic about a future in which buildings are green, healthy, and efficient. "The technology has matured and it's just becoming easier every year. There are more examples out there . . . people can look around and kick the tires . . . they can see for themselves what's happening. There are many shades of green and there are many opportunities, regardless of whether it's a very modest project or a larger project. People should feel good about that."

Systems Thinking

Jason wants buildings to be more like flowers. Amy Thompson yearns for buildings that are more like complex modern aircraft. Amy is an associate professor-in-residence of systems engineering and the associate director of academic programs with the United Technologies Corporation Institute of Advanced Systems Engineering (UTC-IASE) at the University of Connecticut. She currently teaches model-based systems engineering and coordinates the online graduate programs in advanced systems engineering for the UTC-IASE.[9]

"We need to look at energy efficiency in buildings from a systems perspective," Amy says, "using practices and methods that we've practiced for years in the aerospace industry and other industries with complex systems. We can apply those methods to design and operate buildings. We can reduce operating costs and reduce energy consumption. We can also improve the overall satisfaction and comfort levels of the people who live and work in buildings."

Most important, she says, "when we apply systems engineering, we can design reliability and resilience into more of our buildings." In a world of increasingly extreme weather events, those qualities will be essential for ensuring our safety and economic survival.

Thinking about buildings as individual, stand-alone structures reflects an outmoded and unrealistic view of the world. Ideally, the built environment should be viewed as a "system of systems," a vast network of interrelated and interconnected buildings, each interacting with its environment, responding to changes in weather, and pooling information in real time with neighboring buildings.

"We need to design and optimize at a macro level," Amy says. In other words, it's not enough for a single individual building to be smart, efficient, economical, and eco-friendly. All buildings should share these characteristics—*and* they should be interconnected within their corporations or communities, and with external sources of information such as power grids and weather data providers.

For example, imagine the financial and environmental benefits if every building shared information with a regional power grid and could buy or sell energy automatically based on real-time demand and pricing, both of which can vary widely over the course of a typical day.

All of this, of course, would create levels of complexity and uncertainty that would be unthinkable for many architects, developers, investors, and government regulators. Yet I see hope for a systems engineering approach taking hold in our building industry. The aerospace industry deals routinely with high levels of complexity and uncertainty, and that hasn't stopped it from designing and building amazing machines that are safe, reliable, and efficient.

Some large corporations and universities already view their campuses as portfolios of interconnected structures and have developed programs to optimize operational efficiencies across multiple buildings. My hunch is that the systems approach will become more common as the benefits of systems thinking become more widely known and organizations generally grow more accustomed to managing higher levels of uncertainty.

What Makes a Good Building?

As always, the devil is in the details. A "good" building is more than just energy efficient, eco-friendly, and equipped with sensors. Location matters, too. From my perspective, a good building is within easy walking or wheeling distance of a public transportation hub. You shouldn't be forced to drive to a building; that runs counter to the idea of using energy wisely.

Good buildings collect rainwater, recycle their trash, compost waste from toilets, and convert excess heat into usable forms of energy. In addition to charging stations for EVs, good buildings have bike racks. They also have fitness centers and cafés with healthy foods. Increasingly, they are constructed with materials that don't emit toxic fumes or pose health risks to occupants.[10]

A good building exemplifies the idea of a "circular economy" in which garbage and pollution are minimized; the building's systems are regenerative by design, rather than wasteful. In a good building, practically everything is insulated: walls, doors, windows, roofs, pipes, and ductwork. Every device that consumes energy is continually monitored by an integrated building management system. All of the building's individual systems (e.g., lighting, water, HVAC, pumps, generators) share real-time data and can be remotely controlled.

Yet there's more to a good building than updated features and advanced capabilities. A good building also reflects the mindset of its owner. "A good building has an owner who genuinely cares about its operation and isn't viewing it simply as an annuity," says Hugh Seaton, a building information systems expert and the author of *The Construction Technology Handbook*. "A good building is designed for the people who live or work in it. A good building is built to sustain life. It's not just a box of concrete, steel, and glass."

I agree with Hugh. Whether a building is "good" or "bad" depends largely on the goals and intentions of its owner. The best buildings are owned or operated by men and women who genuinely care about their buildings and want to provide the best possible experiences for the people living or working in them.

The Green Building Alliance has an excellent collection of resources on its website (https://www.go-gba.org/resources/building-product-certifications/), and I urge you to spend some time browsing through the list of green building certifications, rating systems, and labels.

Getting Down to the Nitty Gritty

I am a business leader, educator, attorney, and parent. I am no stranger to hard work and long hours. In my life, I have faced many "impossible" challenges and managed to overcome them.

In almost every instance, patience and perseverance were my keys to success. As they say in the military, "The difficult we do immediately; the impossible takes a little longer."

There is no magic formula for improving how energy is used in the built environment. Every building, every business, and every home is different. A solution that works in one place won't work in another. But here's a simple statement from the US Environmental Protection Agency that I always keep in mind:

> *"For a typical office building, energy represents 30 percent of the variable costs and constitutes the single largest controllable operating cost."*[11]

Energy efficiency takes effort. You crawl around with a flashlight looking for cracks in walls. You poke around in dark rooms searching for hidden equipment that might be drawing power. You stand on ladders and peer into drop ceilings hunting for clues and hoping you're not breathing asbestos dust.

You spend hours poring over receipts, invoices, and tax returns, looking for mistakes and oversights. You spend days, weeks, and months researching websites of government agencies.

When I visit a customer in the field, I look at everything from the window panes to the thermostats. In addition to inspecting machinery and equipment, I look at doors, stairwells, floors, ceilings, and walls. I get a sense of what's going on and how they're using energy. I ask myself, "What's wrong with this picture and how can I help them reduce the amount of energy they use, become more productive, and save money?"

I also reflect on the totality of their operations. Are they running three shifts? Is their industry tightly regulated? Are they aware of tax credits and other financial incentives? Many of my clients are rightfully enmeshed in the details of their business. That can make it hard for them to see opportunities for using energy more efficiently. In my role as an energy consultant, I can step back and take a holistic view of their operations. Taking that step back gives me a sense of perspective that I can use to help a client.

Digging Deeper, Searching for Clues

Saving energy involves a surprising amount of physical labor, grunt work, and sleepless nights. There are periods of utter bewilderment followed by momentary flashes of inspiration and insight.

I also have to constantly remind myself that people don't purposefully waste energy. For the most part, the people who hire me are intelligent, capable, and conscientious. They care deeply about their families and their communities. They want to do the right thing, but they are driven by the need to run their organizations productively and cost-effectively.

Typically, they are trained in business or finance. They aren't physicists or electrical engineers. It takes an unusual combination of high-level skills and hands-on experience to become an expert in energy efficiency. It would be unrealistic to expect someone who isn't specifically trained in this field to understand how all the moving parts fit together.

For example, some manufacturing plants and mills still use traditional DC (direct current) motors in their various operations. DC motors are hot, noisy, and can be less efficient than AC (alternating current) motors in some situations. Yet facility managers and their crews often resist switching to them. Why do they resist? They resist because DC motors represent familiar technology. When you're running a manufacturing assembly line, unscheduled downtime can be ruinous. As a result, you stick with what you know. From the perspective of a plant manager whose livelihood depends on uninterrupted throughput, it makes sense to rely on tried-and-true technologies such as DC.

Or does it? When we dug deeper, we found that plant managers often rejected AC (alternating current) motors because they were unaware of advances in digital control technology that can make AC a far more reasonable choice than DC.

For decades, plant managers preferred DC motors because they could be run at various speeds. AC motors, however, were much less flexible in terms of speed. Today, however, an AC motor can be equipped with a variable frequency drive, which means you can vary its speed. The added flexibility enables you to conserve energy, improve productivity, and boost output.

Here's another factor for consideration: Due to their basic design, all electric motors draw some power that cannot be converted into useful energy. This wasted power is commonly referred to as kilo volt ampere reactive (KVAR). KVAR is important because utilities charge their customers a penalty for wasted power, which puts unnecessary loads on their equipment and increases demand.

DC motors start slowly and create more resistance than AC motors, which can be started more efficiently and produce less KVAR. If you're running a plant with lots of DC motors and you're not keeping a close eye on the resulting KVAR, you could wind up paying thousands or tens of thousands of dollars in penalties to your utility company.

Most of us never consider the finer details of our relationships with the utilities that supply our power. Unless there's a power outage, we turn on our lights, appliances, and devices without giving them a second thought. That's natural, and it's a testament to the overall reliability of energy infrastructure. But our collective lack of awareness will lead to unpleasant and unnecessarily expensive consequences down the road.

For many companies and organizations, pesky details such as KVAR can make huge differences in net earnings. I have absolutely no memory of learning about KVAR in high school or college, but it's become one of the first metrics I check when I review the power use of a factory or production mill.

Of course, there's a lot more to energy efficiency than KVAR. Sometimes you can save energy by making better use of a resource that you already have in abundance.

One of my early customers was a major food processor. At the end of each workday, the plant was shut down for a rigorous overnight cleaning. Every inch of the plant, including all the machinery, was meticulously washed and carefully disinfected. The cleaning crew used a mixture of hot water and caustic detergents. It was an expensive and arduous process.

First, they had to heat 40,000 gallons of water every night. Then they had to apply the mixture of water and detergents to every surface, followed by a thorough rinsing. Then they had to dispose of the water and detergents in an environmentally responsible manner.

When I toured the facility, I couldn't help noticing the enormous steel kettles they used for cooking. The kettles were heated with steam made in a special system that was placed on stand-by mode while the facility was idle. That gave me an idea, which soon became an energy-efficiency project. We recommended using the unused steam to clean the facility. Not only did the company save money by eliminating the cost of heating 40,000 gallons of water every night, they significantly reduced the time and labor necessary to clean the plant because steam is far more effective than hot water for cleaning. And the need for caustic detergents went away, because steam also disinfects as it cleans.

A couple of years ago we were hired by the owners of a high-rise office building that had been designed and built in the 1970s. The building was attractive and well situated, yet it clearly reflected the design and construction methods of an earlier era. It had electric baseboard heating, thousands of incandescent and older-style fluorescent lights, and more than a thousand single-pane windows. Each floor had only two thermostats to control heating and cooling, making it virtually impossible to maintain comfortable temperatures across an entire floor.

Putting it bluntly, this beautiful building was an energy hog. Our job was lowering its astronomical energy costs. We began by installing two-panel inserts over the existing windows, which meant that every window now had three panes of glass. The window inserts lowered energy costs by making it easier to cool the building in the summer and heat it in the winter.

We replaced the old lights with light emitting diodes (LEDs), which provide light that is easier on the eyes and require considerably less power. We recommended installing a building management system that automatically controls the building's various systems, reducing heating and cooling costs dramatically.

In addition to saving money, the improvements have made the building more attractive to prospective buyers and boosted its market value. Its workspaces were more comfortable, and the tenants were happier.

I love stories such as these because they show you can solve difficult problems by applying a combination of knowledge, experience, and creativity. You don't need to be a genius. You just need to look at situations with fresh eyes and an open mind.

Endnotes

1. https://www.eia.gov/tools/faqs/faq.php?id=86&t=1
2. https://www.worldgbc.org/sites/default/files/UNEP%20188_GABC_en%20%28web%29.pdf
3. https://flowcharts.llnl.gov/content/assets/images/energy/us/Energy_US_2019.png
4. https://www.ase.org/initiatives/buildings
5. https://living-future.org/lbc/
6. http://mclennan-design.com/
7. https://www.chathamhouse.org/sites/default/files/publications/2018-06-13-making-concrete-change-cement-lehne-preston-exec-sum.pdf

8. https://bullittcenter.org/building/building-features/tall-timbers/
9. https://utc-iase.uconn.edu/person/amy-thompson/#
10. https://transparency.perkinswill.com/
11. https://www.epa.gov/sites/production/files/2017-06/documents/ee_municipal_operations.pdf

Chapter 2

Stabilizing Demand

Your energy costs depend largely on how much energy you use. Yet there is another critical factor in the equation. It's called demand stabilization, and it's incredibly important, both to your checkbook and to our planet's long-term health.

Why is stabilizing demand essential? Let's take a step back and look at the big picture. In the United States, we take electricity for granted. When we flip a switch or push a button, we expect whatever device we're using to begin working instantaneously.

But most of us never think about what's going on behind the curtain. Generating electricity and delivering it safely to your home or business is a complex endeavor involving thousands of interrelated processes working together smoothly and seamlessly.

Here's an excerpt from the US Energy Information Administration website that summarizes the complexity of the task:

> *Electricity is generated at power plants and moves through a complex system, sometimes called the grid, of electricity substations, transformers, and power lines that connect electricity producers and consumers. Most local grids are interconnected for reliability and commercial purposes, forming larger, more dependable networks that enhance the coordination and planning of electricity supply.*[1]

In the United States, the entire electricity grid consists of hundreds of thousands of miles of high-voltage power lines and millions of miles of low-voltage power lines with distribution transformers that connect thousands of power plants to hundreds of millions of electricity customers all across the country.

Here's a question to consider: How does the energy ecosystem respond to our collective expectation that electricity will be available instantaneously and whenever we need it? The simple answer is that the various players in the ecosystem keep a close watch on how much electricity is consumed and do their utmost to make certain there's always enough energy available to meet the peak demand.

In a world of unlimited resources, there's nothing wrong with that model. But we don't live in that kind of world. Our energy-producing resources are finite and have costs associated with them. Our atmosphere, which is a natural resource itself, isn't capable of absorbing unlimited amounts of carbon dioxide and other greenhouse gases. The world has changed since the early days of electricity. Slowly but steadily, the energy ecosystem is evolving into something that's more flexible, less centralized, and considerably more complicated than the simplified model just described.

The grids and the power companies are aware of all this, and they understand the consequences of allowing supply to blindly follow ever-rising demand. The grids actively encourage the power companies to accurately forecast demand and to avoid spikes in use. The power companies also have programs for stabilizing demand and discouraging spikes in use by their customers.

Remember, the power companies are required by law to make electricity available to their customers. The problem, however, is that the power companies are never sure precisely how much electricity they will have to supply. If your power use spikes in June, the power company will make sure they supply you with enough power to cover a similar spike in July.

Here's where it gets interesting: if you are a commercial customer and you don't use that extra power that's been generated for you, the power company will charge you an additional fee. In a very tangible way, you will be penalized for not using the extra power. Ideally, that should make you think twice about letting your power use spike.

That scenario explains why every business needs to understand the value of stabilizing demand. It's not just a matter of common sense—it's a matter of dollars and cents! The money you pay the power company in additional fees can add up fast, reducing your profits significantly.

The amount of the fees varies by region and locality; they also vary by rate class, which is a designation power companies use to classify different types of customers. Yes, there are plenty of confusing details, but the simple truth is that stabilizing your demand will save you money.

There's also a philosophical dimension that's worth pondering. I spoke recently with Sandeep Nimmagadda, director of the Global Laboratory Energy Asset Management & Manufacturing (GLEAMM) project at Texas Tech University, in Lubbock, Texas. GLEAMM works with the commercial sector to "test, certify, research, develop, and support the manufacturing of electrical grid technologies and next-generation power electronic devices."[2] In our conversation, Sandeep made an interesting comment that stayed with me: "For the last several decades, we have been designing systems where the generator basically follows the load."

Put differently, we've created an energy culture in which suppliers are expected to meet any kind of demand, no matter how large or how small. But we're on the cusp of a paradigm shift. Alternative energy sources and advanced digital technologies, combined with our growing awareness of climate change risks, are accelerating a reversal in the way we look at energy.

Within a short span of time, our traditional approach to energy will be stood on its head. Instead of generators following loads, we will have loads following generators. This isn't merely a philosophical issue; the impact on our lives will be profound and long-lasting.

Techniques and Strategies for Stabilizing Demand

There are several ways for commercial users to stabilize demand and reduce spikes in energy consumption:

- Run equipment during off-peak hours.
- Have a battery that will draw energy from alternative sources or from the grid during off-peak hours and supply energy to your business during peak hours.

- Install fuel cells that will generate electricity and/or heat from chemical reactions.

- Install a combined heat and power system that generates electricity *and* useful heating and cooling. This is commonly referred to as *cogeneration* or *trigeneration.*

- Build a microgrid that will enable you to use diverse sources of energy (such as wind, solar, thermal, waste biomass, battery, or fuel cell) that can be used during peak hours or during power outages.

None of those solutions are new, exotic, or particularly difficult to implement. Microgrids are becoming an increasingly common choice for hospitals, schools, office parks, sports arenas, data centers, municipal waste treatment facilities, military installations, and prisons. Major manufacturers such as Siemens, Schneider Electric, S&C Electric, and Schweitzer Engineering Laboratories are leading suppliers of microgrid controls and related technologies. It's fair to say that microgrids are a fast-growing segment of the power industry, and it seems likely their popularity will continue for the foreseeable future.

Islands of Energy

The US Department of Energy Microgrid Exchange Group defines a microgrid as "a group of interconnected loads and distributed energy resources within clearly defined electrical boundaries that acts as a single controllable entity with respect to the grid. A microgrid can connect and disconnect from the grid to enable it to operate in both grid-connected or island-mode."[3]

The concept of "islanding" is important to grasp. From my perspective, microgrids play an especially valuable role in our modern energy ecosystem because they can operate within the grid *and* function independently from the grid, depending on the situation.

For example, a microgrid can be used for stabilizing demand during normal times and as a backup source of power during emergencies. Microgrids can be configured to use renewable or sustainable energy sources (e.g., solar, wind, thermal, and biomass), which makes them a good choice for organizations that are striving to reduce their use of traditional fossil fuels.

"A microgrid is very similar to a large grid, but it has a smaller footprint," says Elisa Wood, editor-in-chief of *Microgrid Knowledge*, a provider of news on microgrids and distributed energy resources.[4] "What really distinguishes a microgrid is that it is able to island from the grid. It can either operate connected to the grid or it can island from the grid. That's definitely a distinguishing characteristic and probably its most important characteristic."

The "brain" of the microgrid, Wood explains, is the microgrid controller, which processes information and optimizes the functions of the microgrid's various components in real time. This is another aspect in which microgrids represent a genuine break with the past: a microgrid's controller enables it to respond to changing conditions on a moment-to-moment basis.

Traditional systems, which typically depend on huge spinning turbines to generate power, are either running or not running—there isn't much subtlety in their basic operating principles. It takes a while for a traditional turbine generator to spin up to speed, and once it's spinning at speed, the idea is to let it keep spinning.

Thanks to its controller, a microgrid can be highly adjustable and responsive. Moreover, the controller can be programmed to optimize the use of available resources. "An advanced controller knows the price of electricity on the grid and can determine whether it's cheaper for the microgrid to use its on-site resources or to buy power from the grid," Elisa says. "At certain times of the day, when grid power is very cheap, the microgrid might ramp down its generation and start buying power from the grid."

Microgrid operators can choose which parameters to optimize. "Perhaps the operator's goals are sustainability and reducing carbon emissions," Elisa says. "Then the operator would program the microgrid to make sure that at any point in the day, it's always choosing the power sources that have the lowest emissions."

Microgrids also ensure continuity during power outages. "If a manufacturing business loses its electricity for a few minutes, the cost can be tremendous," says Elisa. "I wrote about a milk production facility in northern Virginia that has a microgrid because they are required by law to shut down and clean everything if they lose power even momentarily."

Generating Buzz

The rising popularity of microgrids often obscures their complexity. Today's microgrids are carefully designed assemblies of sophisticated subcomponents that must be tuned and tinkered with to produce optimal results. But that wasn't always the case.

"Nowadays, there's a lot of buzz around microgrids, and deservedly so," says Tim Kelley, director of advance hybrid microgrids at Russelectric, a Siemens subsidiary based in Massachusetts. "The original microgrids were generators, usually diesel, that would supply emergency power during blackouts. Most of the time, they just sat there and did nothing unless a hurricane came though and shut down the grid."

Prior to the Northeast blackout of 1965, in which thirty million people lost power for twelve hours, many facilities relied on portable, truck-mounted generators for emergency backup power. The blackout revealed the limitations of relying on relatively small numbers of diesel generators to handle a widespread emergency and spurred interest in the development of more reliable backup systems. In the aftermath of the blackout, new government regulations required critical facilities such as hospitals, airports, and water treatment plants to install on-site emergency backup generators. Those early systems were the ancestors of today's microgrids.

Despite subsequent blackouts, however, microgrids receded from the public eye and remained a niche phenomenon, relegated to "mission critical" or essential services facilities, with diesel generators being the primary technology and designed to serve a single purpose: emergency backup power.

More recently, a convergence of forces (such as rising awareness of climate change, advances in digital control technologies, availability and rapidly declining cost of alternative energy sources, and regulatory changes) has spurred new life into the microgrid market, with microgrids composed of multiple generating technologies and providing multiple benefits instead of just one.

The renewed interest in microgrids is also driven by economics. Over the past dozen years, the availability of alternative energy sources such as wind, solar, and battery power has risen substantially and the costs associated with them have fallen dramatically. As a result, hybrid microgrids that use multiple sources of energy to generate power are now practical from an economic perspective.

"The prices of alternative energy sources and related technologies have declined dramatically over the past decade, 80 to 90 percent for solar and energy storage, and these prices continue to fall," Tim says. "In addition to that, you've had a lot of policy changes, usually on a state-by-state basis, that provide incentives for solar and storage. And two years ago, the Federal Energy Regulatory Commission (FERC) issued Rule 841 requiring all the regional power grids to open up their power markets to energy storage devices or batteries that are 100 kW or larger."

The FERC ruling is a meaningful step forward in the evolution of our energy ecosystem. In the past, you could use your batteries or storage devices to provide backup power and clip your peak demand. But the FERC ruling enables you to also sell stored power to the grid. From my perspective, that's a game changer. It genuinely feels as though we are on the doorstep of a new and exciting era in energy economics.

"Costs are coming down on these alternative technologies to the point that they are absolutely more than competitive with utility power, and very often cheaper than utility power, in many parts of the country," Tim says. "At the same time, you also have a trend on the policy side that makes it easier to get more value out of these distributed energy resources."

Wider Adoption, but Hurdles Remain

Unquestionably, microgrids have become a critical part of our evolving energy ecosystem. I urge you to visit the Connecticut Department of Energy and Environmental Protection website[5] and scroll through the list of microgrid projects currently underway across the state.[6] Many states publish similar lists, and I believe you will be pleasantly surprised by the number of projects that are in the works.

That said, microgrids still face obstacles. One of the primary barriers to greater adoption of microgrids is their sheer complexity. "In the old days, microgrids had diesel generators designed to do one thing: turn on when the electric grid turned off. The market has decades of experience building and operating these microgrids," Tim explains. "Today, a microgrid can have multiple power sources providing multiple benefits, including emergency backup power, carbon reduction, energy cost reduction, and more. Integrating different technologies and getting them to work harmoniously together for different purposes is much more challenging. It's all technically feasible and financially practical, but there are a lot of moving parts to get your head around."

After your microgrid is up and running, you may feel a strong temptation to test its strength and explore its vast potential. That's when you're likely to confront local regulatory issues. "Let's say you have a microgrid on one property and you want to use it to generate electricity for some buildings on another property across the street," Tim says. "Then you're opening up a big can of worms because most towns and cities have laws against running power lines across a street unless you're a utility."

I like how Tim puts the opportunities and challenges of operating microgrids into perspective. As an attorney, I wish the laws and regulations governing power were more uniform and less confusing. Each state has its own regulations and each town has its own set of rules. As I mentioned previously, I'm in favor of self-determination and I'm not a fan of big government. But our nation's inability to create a comprehensive set of energy regulations is turning into a strategic weakness, which is troubling. I'll revisit this topic in Chapter 4.

No Surprises

Our brains are wired to hate surprises. We enjoy suspense and we are entertained by the prospect of modest danger, but surprise itself usually produces a negative emotional response. The energy ecosystem shares our human aversion to surprises but responds by producing additional costs. The magnitude of those costs can be extraordinary.

Imagine a week in October in which the temperatures are unusually warm and everyone in the Northeast turns on their air conditioners to keep cool. The unexpected additional demand for electricity will likely catch the local power companies by surprise, and they might need to rely on backup generation systems that run on fuels that are both dirtier and more expensive than the natural gas they usually burn to make electricity. Or they might begin drawing more power from their grid, which might in turn have to draw power from another grid to supply the sudden spike in demand. In any event, the costs of these fallback maneuvers will be large in terms of money spent and damage to the environment.

When you use energy can have an enormous impact on your total energy costs. Timing isn't everything, but it is major factor. Here's a basic rule-of-thumb: It's better to use energy when demand is low. As a result, it pays to know when demand is high and to avoid running power-hungry equipment during those hours. The hours in which peak use typically occurs is printed on your power bill, so there's no excuse for not knowing.

In the near future, the grid will send signals to you in real time indicating when peak use is occurring. Eventually, many of your devices and systems will be interconnected and integrated with the grid. Essentially, they will function in collaboration with the grid. The combination of advanced reasoning capabilities and access to real-time information from the grid will enable our devices and systems to decide for themselves when to use or not to use energy. And they won't be making simple on-off decisions: depending on how they're programmed, they will be capable of making incremental changes in use to optimize a range of variables including costs, efficiency, sustainability, and zero-carbon emissions.

For example, a smart energy system will have the capability to choose when to run devices and machines, choose the type of energy used to run them, and monitor their performance in real time to make sure they are running efficiently. And smart buildings, smart factories, and smart schools won't just consume energy—they will optimize their use of energy and return unused or excess energy to the community around them or to the grid itself.

Endnotes

1. https://www.eia.gov/energyexplained/electricity/delivery-to-consumers.php
2. https://gleamm.org/about/
3. https://building-microgrid.lbl.gov/microgrid-definitions
4. https://microgridknowledge.com/about/
5. https://portal.ct.gov/DEEP/Energy/Microgrid-Grant-and-Loan/Microgrid-Grant-and-Loan-Program
6. https://portal.ct.gov/-/media/DEEP/energy/MicrogridsProjectAwardTrackingAllProjectspdf.pdf

Chapter 3

Why Batteries Matter

Today, most of us are passive consumers of energy produced in large power plants. In the very near future, however, most of us will also become energy producers. The traditional one-to-many model of energy distribution will evolve rapidly into a many-to-many network of users and suppliers.

Imagine this scenario: when you arrive home, you plug your electric vehicle (EV) into your home battery storage system. Your home system will read the status of the battery in your EV and determine if it needs additional charging or if it has more energy than you're likely to need in the next couple of hours.

Your home system is connected to a large network of providers and consumers. If your system detects that you have more energy in your car battery than you need, it will reach out to the network and find out if there's any demand for your excess power. It will also check the price that buyers are willing to pay. If the price is right, it will sell your power and your account will be credited automatically. Voila, you've made money by simply plugging your EV into a wall socket in your garage!

Similar to how the internet enabled anyone to become a publisher, this new internet of electricity will enable anyone to become a power supplier.

Battery Culture

Without much fanfare, a battery culture is emerging. Some of what's driving the battery culture are globally popular consumer products such as smartphones, laptops, and electric vehicles, all of which run on lithium-ion batteries.

The downside of lithium-ion batteries is their weight and cost. The upside is their efficiency: A one-kilogram lithium-ion battery can store up to 150 watt-hours of electricity. Weight can be a problem if the battery is powering your car, laptop, or phone. But weight isn't an issue when the battery is installed in a home or commercial building. I predict that within a short time span, most buildings will have battery storage systems and that many of those systems will be connected to the grid, enabling a two-way exchange of energy.

If you're passionate about energy, the next five or six years will be exciting times. We'll see amazing developments that will both democratize and complicate our relationships with energy. Clearly, the clean energy trend will continue and accelerate. At the same time, we'll see far less use of dirty fuels such as coal and oil. We'll have many more choices about which kinds of energy we want to consume. Digital information technologies and advanced data science techniques will enable us to share electricity across networks, creating vast new opportunities for people all over the world.

Batteries will play a major role in the shift from centralized to distributed energy systems. Our power grids were born during an era in which bigger invariably meant better. Utilities were granted monopoly status because there didn't seem to be an alternative way for ensuring that power would always be available whenever people needed it.

Today, we have alternatives and we have the motivation to use them. Clean and renewable energy sources are good for the environment and good for the economy. People generally agree that clean energy is an achievable goal. We're still arguing over the best ways to achieve that goal, but I'm highly confident that the goal is within reach.

Enabling Energy Evolution

Electricity is a perishable product. It's here one moment and gone the next. Most of our electricity is generated on demand and consumed within fractions of a second. When our grid system was set up, storage was not a priority. Today, storage is moving front and center.

Storage is important now for two reasons:

- Stabilizing demand
- Using variable energy sources (such as wind and solar) at scale

There are several ways to store power, but the most familiar method is battery storage. Research teams at companies
and universities are racing to develop a new generation of
batteries that are powerful, reliable, cost-effective, and safe.
We should be rooting for those research teams to succeed,
because the quality of our lives going forward may depend
on our ability to produce good batteries in large numbers.

Stabilizing Demand

Batteries enable businesses and individuals to store excess
energy and use it as an alternative to grid power during
peak hours, which is beneficial to energy customers because
many electric utilities impose extra fees for using during peak
power. It's also good for the environment because it reduces
the need for utilities to rely on "peaker" power plants, which
typically run on fossil fuels, to supply energy during hours
when demand for electricity is unusually high.

Peaker plants can have ruinous effects on the health of
people living in the communities around them. "Combustion
of fossil fuels at peaker plants emits localized pollutants such
as nitrogen oxides (NOx) and sulfur dioxide (SO_2), which are
both directly harmful and can contribute to the secondary
formation of ozone and fine particulate matter (PM2.5). Peak-
ers, particularly older ones, emit a higher level of pollutants
relative to the electricity they generate . . . deploying battery
storage to replace peaker plants could result in a significant
reduction in these criteria air pollutants and improve public health outcomes," according to a report from the Peak
Coalition.[1]

Using Variable Energy Sources at Scale

Even our most powerful supercomputers can't predict when the wind will blow and when clouds will pass in front of the sun. One of the obstacles that made it difficult to replace traditional energy fuels with wind and solar energy sources was their variability; we simply could not depend on them to generate power steadily and consistently every day of the year. But that obstacle is quickly vanishing.

Increasingly, batteries enable us to store energy from clean and renewable sources and use it when we need it. Batteries can serve as a bank for energy, saving megawatts of power from variable sources that would otherwise be lost.

That's why battery storage is an essential part of the evolving energy story. Ideally, more battery storage will translate into more power generated from renewable sources and fewer power plants using nonrenewable fuels.

The outlook for batteries is bright. The cost of battery systems, along with the cost of wind and solar energy systems, has been dropping steadily for years, falling 87 percent from 2010 to 2019.[2] "Batteries keep getting better. Average battery energy density is rising at 4 to 5 percent per year and new chemistries are hitting the market," according to the Electric Vehicle Outlook,[3] an annual long-term forecast compiled by BloombergNEF.[4]

The combination of batteries and renewable energy is no longer a fringe concept; it's become widely accepted across the energy industry.

In what's been described as "a turning point" for renewable energy, the largest battery storage system in the United

States connected to the California electricity grid in June 2020, adding 62.5 megawatts (MW) of storage to the system.[5]

The battery system will enable the grid to store solar power generated during daylight hours and distribute it later when needed. The additional storage capacity is impressive, yet it's still a drop in the bucket: California will probably need 15,000 MW of battery storage to meet its carbon-free energy goal by 2045.[6] Nevertheless, California's achievement is a critical step in the right direction, and the state has plans to add more storage capacity over time.

"The pool of renewable energy will continue increasing," says Peter Asmus, a research analyst who focuses on the power industry and emerging energy distribution networks. "You're seeing states, corporations, and utilities with 100 percent renewable energy goals. The portion of power supply that comes from renewables will keep growing."

Asmus foresees a dramatic growth in energy generated by small sources such as microgrids. Soon, he says, "the amount of energy the world gets from small sources will be greater than the amount of energy we get from large-scale sources and the gap between those two will grow over time."

A world of small and distributed energy resources will require new techniques and technologies to orchestrate highly complex, fast-moving relationships at every level, from regional transmission grid operators to homeowners with rooftop solar panels. The power systems of tomorrow will need artificial intelligence, machine learning, edge computing, and high-speed communications networks to stay ahead of energy demands in real time.

Electrifying Energy

Let's do some time traveling and take a quick trip into the early decades of the twentieth century. If your great-grandparents lived in a city or town, their home probably had electric lights and appliances. If they lived on a farm, chances are good they had no electricity and therefore no electric appliances. They had no refrigerators or washing machines. When they needed water for cooking or washing, they had to pull it up from a well and carry it back to the house in large heavy buckets. When the sun set, they lit candles or lanterns. Most likely, they sat outside for a while watching the stars and then went to bed.

The Rural Electrification Act of 1936 changed the lives of millions of Americans by bringing electricity to areas that had been considered too remote for electric service. There is an absolutely heartbreaking chapter in Robert Caro's (1981) multivolume biography of Lyndon Johnson in which he describes the hardships endured by farm families in the generations before electricity was widely available.

Electrification transformed our culture profoundly, setting the stage for decades of strong economic growth and prosperity. In retrospect, bringing electricity to virtually every community in the United States seems like a no-brainer. But in the 1930s, the idea was revolutionary.

I believe we're on the edge of a similar revolution powered by electricity. In this revolution, electrification opens the door to a future in which less energy is wasted and more energy is used effectively. Electrification will also play a key role in reducing carbon emissions.

Electrifying the transportation sector, for example, would result in significantly less CO_2 being released into the air from traditional internal combustion engines.[7] It would also substantially reduce harmful particulates that can promote disease, aggravate existing health conditions, and shorten life expectancies.[8]

Nick Nigro, founder of Atlas Public Policy,[9] sees a direct connection between electric transportation and decarbonization. "Electrifying transportation is the single most important step we can take," Nick says. "Regardless, when you look at the life cycle emissions of an EV, it is always better than its conventional counterpart . . . the EV is going to beat the conventional vehicle pound-for-pound on a carbon basis because the EV itself is so much more efficient at turning potential energy into kinetic energy."

As more power companies shift to clean renewable fuels for generating electricity, the environmental advantages of EVs are multiplied. "There's a widescale effort to decarbonize (electric power generation), so it's kind of a 'two-fer' . . . you're leveraging the decarbonization of the power sector, which is the power source for the battery in the EV," Nick explains.

Here are two additional benefits of EVs: because most people charge them at night during off-peak hours, they put less of a strain on the grid than if they were charged during peak hours. And because the winds are generally stronger at night, they can generate more electricity at night than during the day. "As we add more wind power onto the grid, there's a real opportunity for EVs to absorb that additional nighttime capacity because they're almost certainly parked overnight somewhere near a power outlet," Nick says.

EVs are no longer a niche market. Here are some fascinating stats quoted from BloombergNEF's Electric Vehicle Outlook:[10]

- *Passenger EV sales jumped from 450,000 in 2015 to 2.1 million in 2019.*
- *By 2022 there will be over 500 different EV models available globally.*
- *By the mid-2020s EVs reach up-front price parity— without subsidies—with internal combustion vehicles in most segments, but there is wide variation by region.*
- *By 2040, over half of all passenger vehicles sold will be electric.*
- *EVs across all segments are already displacing 1 million barrels of oil demand per day.*
- *EVs and fuel cell vehicles reduce road CO_2 emissions by 2.57Gt a year by 2040—and are set for much larger reductions thereafter.*

Autonomous self-driving EVs may bring even greater benefits to society, because it's fair to assume that manufacturers will program their EVs to achieve maximum battery efficiency. Self-driving vehicles could "end up with energy savings of as much as 10 percent simply by making better decisions about braking, accelerating, and turning than human drivers," writes Akshat Rathi, a London-based reporter for Bloomberg News.

There is a strong connection among renewable energy sources, batteries, stabilizing demand, and EVs. At this point, each of those phenomena are related and moving together in a positive upward trend. This convergence bodes well for our economy and our environment.

Endnotes

1. https://www.cleanegroup.org/wp-content/uploads/Dirty-Energy-Big-Money.pdf
2. https://about.bnef.com/blog/battery-pack-prices-fall-as-market-ramps-up-with-market-average-at-156-kwh-in-2019/
3. https://about.bnef.com/electric-vehicle-outlook/
4. https://about.bnef.com/
5. https://www.utilitydive.com/news/largest-battery-resource-connects-caiso-system/581540/
6. https://www.bloomberg.com/news/articles/2020-07-13/biggest-u-s-battery-storage-system-connects-to-california-grid
7. https://www.energy.gov/eere/electricvehicles/reducing-pollution-electric-vehicles
8. https://www.epa.gov/report-environment/greenhouse-gases
9. https://atlaspolicy.com/
10. https://about.bnef.com/electric-vehicle-outlook/

Chapter 4

Energy and the Law

Since the new millennium, it's been fashionable for business and technology writers to praise the virtues of disruption, disintermediation, and decentralization. Words such as *disaggregation* and *democratization* are used indiscriminately, creating the dangerous illusion that complex problems can be solved easily by ordinary people with little or no understanding of how complex systems work in the real world.

Anyone who has raised a family or run a business knows that complex problems resist easy solutions. Problems are like onions: you peel away one layer and there's always another layer underneath it.

Take the problem of energy and the law, for example. There are federal regulations governing the transmission of energy resources such as natural gas and electricity. But there is no common set of laws or regulations governing how energy is consumed at the individual level. That's left to the states and municipalities. As a result, there's a large degree of variability.

Our energy laws are a hot mess; they are inconsistent and unpredictable. They create uncertainty, making it difficult for businesses to plan for the future. In some instances, our energy laws conflict with the rights to private property guaranteed by our Constitution. Because the laws for energy are often ambiguous and easily misinterpreted, they can sow the seeds for unanticipated problems in the future.

Let's say I've built a manufacturing plant in one state and I want to expand operations into another state. In a perfect world, the building and energy codes would be roughly similar from one state to another. But in the real world, they can vary widely. The net result is that I can't use the same design and building plans in different municipalities because they are likely to have different building and energy codes.

New York City (NYC), for instance, has a law requiring energy audits. Here's an excerpt from the NYC Mayor's Office of Sustainability website:

Local Law 87 (LL87) mandates that buildings over 50,000 gross square feet undergo periodic energy audit and retro-commissioning measures, as part of the Greener, Greater Buildings Plan (GGBP). The intent of this law is to inform building owners of their energy consumption through energy audits, which are surveys and analyses of energy use, and retro-commissioning, the process of ensuring correct equipment installation and performance.

In addition to benchmarking annual energy and water consumption, energy audits and retro-commissioning will give building owners a much more robust understanding of their buildings' performance, eventually shifting the market towards increasingly efficient, high-performing buildings.[1]

I believe that Local Law 87 is a good and helpful law. Other cities have similar regulations, but they're slightly different. Here's an excerpt from San Francisco's Existing Buildings Ordinance:

San Francisco's Existing Buildings Ordinance applies to existing non-residential buildings with 10,000 square feet or more of space that is heated or cooled and existing multifamily residential buildings with 50,000 square feet or more of space that is heated or cooled. The ordinance has two separate requirements:

Energy Benchmarking—*due annually on April 1**

The building owner must report the total amount of energy that the building uses every year using the US Environmental Protection Agency's free 'ENERGY STAR Portfolio Manager' website. This process is called "energy benchmarking," and the benchmark report must be submitted to the San Francisco Department of the Environment through the Portfolio Manager by April 1st each year.

Energy Audit—*required every 5 years for nonresidential buildings*

The non-residential building owner must ensure the non-residential building receives an energy audit by a qualified energy professional every five years. The professional must hold one of the qualifications approved by the Department of Environment, and must examine the entire building. The audit provides the building owner with a list of specific opportunities to save money and save energy in the building, as well as any rebates that may be available.[2]

Here's a short description of a similar law in Seattle:

Seattle's Energy Benchmarking Program (SMC 22.920) requires owners of non-residential and multifamily buildings (20,000 sf or larger) to track energy performance and annually report to the City of Seattle.[3]

Obviously, the laws in New York City, San Francisco, and Seattle were created to accomplish similar goals, but they're just different enough so that you would need to hire local attorneys and local contractors to help you comply with each city's code. Now imagine what it would be like if you had a business with stores or facilities in multiple locations across the United States.

"We have the idea that energy laws are monolithic and centralized under one umbrella and that energy issues can be solved by a single entity," says Brandon Barnes, senior litigation analyst for the energy sector at Bloomberg Intelligence. "But that's just not the case. We have a multilevel, multitiered system. You have to deal with issues at each level and tier—and that's where you run into a lot of challenges."

Although it may seem as though several federal agencies are "in charge" of energy, their actual authority is limited. For example, the Federal Energy Regulation Commission (FERC) was initially set up to regulate the interstate transmission of electricity, natural gas, and oil.[4] Since its creation in 1977, FERC has been tasked with numerous additional responsibilities, including governing environmental reviews for major federal energy projects. "Congress decided to take another statute, the National Environmental Policy Act (NEPA), and overlay it on top of the original Natural Gas Act certificate requirement," Brandon explains.

The resulting confusion over who's really in charge is the fault of Congress, not the federal agencies, says Brandon. I agree with that assessment. Considering the scope of FERC's role, it does a pretty good job. But it has little genuine authority over local energy issues.

"The dilemma is that we're trying to use outdated regulations and legal schemes to solve modern problems," Brandon says. "For example, one of the reasons that it's hard to fight climate change is that the law doesn't address it directly."

His comments cut to the heart of the matter. We don't have a practical mechanism for holding companies or individuals accountable for climate change and for the damages caused by climate change, such as coastal erosion, severe weather events, unhealthy air, melting glaciers, and dangerously hot summers in parts of the world. As lawyers say, "there's no single throat to choke" when you're trying to assign liability for climate change. Our common law and case law are not effective tools for fighting climate change. Even our federal laws, such as the Clean Air Act, aren't written to deal directly with the effects of climate change.

"For the most part over the years, the courts have decided they don't actually have the authority to find liability here," Brandon says. "If the goal is finding liability or holding companies accountable, the court is not the proper venue right now."

Essentially, the courts have ruled that climate change is a political issue and should be solved in the political arena, not in the courts. That brings us back to the fundamental problem of inconsistency across our many levels of government.

This lack of consistency is deeply woven into the fabric of American culture, but it's become the Achilles' heel of our relationship with energy. It's critical to remember that energy follows the laws of physics. Energy doesn't care about philosophy or politics. It doesn't matter whether you believe in big government or small government—we need consistent energy regulations that will enable us as a society to generate and consume the energy we need, without irrevocably harming the biosphere we inhabit.

We often hear people complaining about "too many laws." As an energy consultant, I'd say the problem in our industry isn't too many laws—the problem is that many of our energy laws are relics of a bygone era. Today, they need a refresh. They need updating, refinement, and modernization.

We also need to accept that many issues cannot be solved purely by writing and applying better laws. There are market forces that must be acknowledged and incorporated into whatever legal solutions we devise.

In other words, the law has to reflect the realities of our economy and our human nature. As human beings, we respond to rewards and punishments. Good laws provide carrots and sticks—you can't have one without the other.

Carbon Dividends

Incentives are a great example of the carrot-and-stick approach. One of the best incentive plans I've seen is the carbon dividend, which provides a cash award to every citizen, no matter how much money they earn or how much fuel they use. It's financed through an up-front tax paid only by companies that bring fossil fuels to market, which makes it easy to administer and invisible to consumers. This is a crucial element of the plan: the dividend is funded by the companies, not by taxpayers.

Here's the cool part: the dividend is divided evenly among all US citizens, with every citizen receiving an annual check or electronic fund transfer (EFT) payment. For many Americans, the annual dividend check will represent a nice chunk of change.

James Boyce, professor emeritus of economics at the University of Massachusetts, introduced me to the idea of the carbon dividend and he's written an excellent book on the topic: *The Case for Carbon Dividends*. The book is short, and I recommend reading it.

The notion of dividing up profits or dividends from the use of public assets isn't an unrealistic or pie-in-the-sky idea. Alaska already has a similar program called the Alaska Permanent Fund. Essentially, the fund collects fees from oil companies and distributes the money to Alaska residents.

Under the program, every Alaskan receives an annual payment. In 2019, the individual payment was $1,606. A family of four received a check for $6,424 and a family of eight received a check for $12,848.

Interestingly, Alaska is one of only two states (the other is Utah) where income inequality is consistently low,[5] and the fund has had no discernable impact on employment—in other words, Alaskans haven't stopped looking for work merely because they receive an annual payout from the fund.[6]

The continuing success of the Alaska Permanent Fund clearly demonstrates that dividend programs can work if they're simple to understand, easy to administer, and perceived as acutely fair.

The fund truly represents a new style of solving difficult problems. It's an effective blend of socialist and libertarian ideas, created by elected officials and corporate executives who weren't afraid to take risks. They rolled the dice, and every Alaskan won. I think we can replicate their success and create a national carbon dividend that delivers a payout to every American.

The Alaska Permanent Fund also shows that genuinely complicated issues can be resolved constructively and fairly. The fund is proof positive that win-win scenarios are possible and preferable to zero-sum games. In a zero-sum game, there's a winner and a loser. The carbon dividend isn't perfect, but the winners will far outnumber the losers.

Alaska's innovative solution is a game-changer in other ways, too. It opens the door to a frank and thorough discussion about who gets to use public property and how much they should pay when they pollute or destroy public property.

Universal Property

Back in 1940, when the United States was still reeling from the impact of the Great Depression, Woody Guthrie wrote "This Land Is Your Land," the song that became the anthem for future generations of Americans who struggled to preserve our natural environments.

Guthrie's song strikes many people today as old-fashioned, but its core concept is just as relevant now as it was in the

twentieth century. Our natural resources are a shared inheritance from previous generations of Americans. In other words,
we have an ownership stake in our natural resources, and we
have a right to exert control over them.

Look up at the sky. The sky is not owned by individuals
or corporations. It's common property, owned by each and
every one of us. We share ownership of the sky. It's our birth-
right as Americans. We, the people, own the sky.

Then why do we allow polluters to use our sky at no cost?
At minimum, they should be paying fees that we can divide
up among ourselves. Remember, the sky belongs to us. It's
our property. This idea of shared ownership isn't social-
ism; it's pure common sense based on thousands of years of
human culture and tradition.

Requiring companies to pay fees when they pollute the air
will incentivize them to become more efficient and to reduce
the levels of pollutants they emit or discharge into our shared
atmosphere. The fees we collect from polluters will be shared
equally among us. Again, everyone will get a payment, either
by check or via EFT.

Peter Barnes has written two useful books about sharing
dividends from fees or taxes collected from users of shared
natural resources and common assets. In *Who Owns the Sky?*
(2001), he argues that we should think about the cash value
of our shared natural resources and stop allowing corporations to use them at no cost.

"We *can and should* turn some of our shared inheritance
into cash," he writes. "This can be done by (1) charging market prices for using our inherited assets, and (2) paying dividends to ourselves as their rightful inheritors" (p. 2).

It's easy to say that Americans are too focused on money, but the truth is that we're not focused enough on it, especially when it comes to giving away trillions of dollars worth of natural resources. If a large private corporation owned the sky, he writes, "it would charge what the market would bear. But we're not so businesslike. We give our assets away without charging a dime" (p. 3).

In *With Liberty and Dividends for All* (2014), he contends that natural resources are co-owned wealth that would enable us to fund steady and reliable streams of income for an increasingly cash-strapped middle class. Taking a page from the Alaska Permanent Fund, we would collect fees from companies that use our resources and distribute the money in the form of cash dividends.

"Paying dividends from wealth we own together is a practical, market-based way to assure the survival of a large middle class" (p. 2), the author writes. He calls the dividends *nonlabor income*, a term that will become increasingly important to our national conversation as automation relentlessly eliminates or replaces jobs performed by human beings.

Most important, from my perspective, is the inherently nonpolitical nature of the case for dividends, which "require no new taxes or government programs; once set up, they're purely market-based" (p. 3), he writes.

Endnotes

1. https://www1.nyc.gov/html/gbee/html/plan/ll87.shtml
2. https://sfenvironment.org/article/san-franciscos-existing
   -commercial-buildings-ordinance
3. http://www.seattle.gov/environment/climate-change/buildings
   -and-energy/energy-benchmarking
4. https://www.ferc.gov/about/what-ferc/what-ferc-does
5. https://www.adn.com/opinions/2017/01/09/why-alaska-is-the
   -most-equal-of-the-states/; https://en.wikipedia.org/wiki/List_of_
   U.S._states_by_Gini_coefficient
6. https://www.alaskapublic.org/2019/10/03/does-alaskas-pfd
   -contribute-to-lower-income-inequality-its-complicated/

Chapter 5

Your Role in Reducing Carbon Output

It's easy to ignore problems when it seems as though someone else will handle them. That's one of the reasons we're not acting collectively to tackle big problems such as climate change and air pollution. On some level, we simply assume that it's not our job.

We assume that eventually, some well-funded organization or omnipotent government agency will step in and make the problems go away. Or we assume that "market economics" will magically solve our problems while simultaneously creating new wealth for savvy investors.

I respectfully disagree with those assumptions. You want to know who's going to solve our problems? Look in the mirror. We've already got the tools and we know how to use them. This chapter will show you how to get started and how to keep going.

Ancient prophets used guilt, shame, and fear to sway their audiences. Those old-fashioned rhetorical techniques aren't my style. When I'm making the case for energy efficiency, I focus on the upside rather than dwell on the downside. Fortunately, there's plenty of upside to talk about.

That said, there is an inescapable link between wealth and carbon output. Bigger is not better, especially from an environmental perspective. If you own a large home, it's probably creating more pollution than your neighbor who owns a small home. The same holds true for automobiles. If you drive a big gas guzzler, you're polluting more than your friend who drives a compact hybrid.

I'm not even talking about crazy-rich super-wealth. Compared to most of the world, the average middle-class American lives like a king or queen. I'm not trying to make you feel bad, I'm just stating the truth. As a general rule, our level of wealth corresponds proportionately to the level of pollution we're producing. There's no way of getting around this, unless we become more efficient and more thoughtful consumers of energy.

Saving money and reducing energy waste are easy when you get into the right mindset. To me, energy efficiency is similar to regular exercise. At first, it seems hard and strange, but after a short time, it becomes a healthy habit and you wonder why you didn't start doing it sooner.

Simple Steps You Can Take Right Now

Let's start with out-of-sight, out-of-mind systems and equipment. How often do you think about your furnace or boiler? Rarely, I bet. They aren't very interesting, and unless they break down, you don't really have to worry about them. But you should be aware that they're probably costing you hundreds and possibly thousands of dollars each year in wasted energy. They're also major sources of air pollution. Older heating systems are dreadfully inefficient, usually operating somewhere between 56 percent and 70 percent efficiency.

So right off the bat, I would recommend replacing your home heating system if it's more than seven years old. Here's the good news, courtesy of the US Department of Energy (DOE):

> *Modern conventional heating systems can achieve efficiencies as high as 98.5%, converting nearly all the fuel to useful heat for your home. Energy efficiency upgrades and a new high-efficiency heating system can often cut your fuel bills and your furnace's pollution output in half. Upgrading your furnace or boiler from 56% to 90% efficiency in an average cold-climate house will save 1.5 tons of carbon dioxide emissions each year if you heat with gas, or 2.5 tons if you heat with oil.*[1]

Don't buy an oversize boiler or furnace. Sometimes a high-efficiency furnace will end up wasting fuel because it's too large for your home. Talk to your heating contractor and make sure you get a furnace or boiler that's just the right size for your home—not too big and not too small.

I recommend buying a high-efficiency sealed-combustion unit, which draws fresh air from the outside of the house and vents exhaust directly outside. Thanks to its design, a sealed-combustion heating unit eliminates wasted heat that would usually be sent up your chimney. It's also cleaner and less likely to create air pollution inside your house than traditional heating systems.

Don't skimp on maintenance. Similar to all types of machines, boilers and furnaces need tending and adjustment from time to time. Ask your heating contractor how often maintenance is required and stick to the schedule. It might cost you a couple of hundred dollars per year, but keeping your heating system properly maintained will save you quite a bit more over the long run.

Take a look at the DOE's Appliance and Equipment Standards Program, which develops and implements minimum energy conservation standards for a wide variety of appliances and equipment. "By 2030, cumulative operating cost savings from all standards in effect since 1987 will reach nearly $2 trillion," according to the DOE.[2]

The DOE's eeCompass[3] program is an incredibly useful resource for evaluating and comparing more than two million appliances. I urge you to visit the eeCompass website and check it out. You will be amazed at the amount of information available there. Honestly, I wish I had taken advantage of resources such as eeCompass when I was building my home because I would have been able to make it much more energy efficient!

Enjoy Creature Comforts without Wasting Energy

I am not by nature an ostentatious person. But I don't mind spending money on creature comforts that I know I will use, such as a hot tub. After a long day at work, I love settling down into my hot tub with a glass of wine. I also know that hot tubs use a lot of energy, which bothers me.

So here's what I do: After getting out of the tub, I set the temperature to "resort mode," which draws just enough power to keep the water warm while I'm at work. When I return home, I set the temperature back to normal, and within twenty minutes the water is hot enough for a relaxing soak.

Here are more suggestions for reducing your carbon footprint easily and painlessly:

- Put everything on a timer. Then you won't have to remember to turn off your devices and appliances when you're not using them because they'll turn off automatically by themselves.

- Replace every bulb or compact fluorescent light in your house with an LED.

- Convert your outdoor lighting to solar.

- If your refrigerator is more than seven years old, scrap it and buy a new one. Newer refrigerators cost less and are much more efficient than older fridges; newer models pay for themselves after a couple of years. Bring your old refrigerator to the town recycling center where it will be disposed of properly. Resist the urge to relocate it to your basement or garage and use it as some kind of backup. It will be an energy hog no matter where it is, so please just get rid of it.

- Trade in your gasoline-fueled cars, SUVs, and vans for electric or hybrid versions. In the near future, all of us will be driving electric or hybrid vehicles. From my perspective, it makes sense to get ahead of the curve and make the switch now. In some areas, energy providers will reward you for drawing less energy from your home EV charger during periods of peak demand. For example,

Eversource will reward residential customers up to $300 for enrolling their home EV charger in the company's ConnectedSolutions program. Here's a short description of the program from the Eversource website:

The program rewards you for using less energy during periods of peak demand, when others are using more.

For EV chargers, during these periods Eversource will make slight adjustments to decrease the charger's energy use. You will still be able to charge your electric vehicle, but you'll help decrease the strain on Eversource's electric system while lowering your carbon emissions even further.

Your vehicle will charge more slowly, but you'll stay in control and can adjust your charger back to its normal settings if you need to charge more quickly.[4]

Beware of Phantom Loads

Here's another easy way to use less electricity and save money: unplug devices when they're not in use. When you leave computers, chargers, and other household appliances plugged in overnight or while you're away, they will continue to draw small amounts of power. This phenomenon is known by colorful nicknames such as *phantom load, vampire power, ghost load,* and *electric leakage.* No matter what you call it, leaving devices plugged in when you're not using them can add $200 per year to your electricity costs, according to NativeEnergy.[5]

Fighting phantom load doesn't require a lot of work. I recommend plugging your electronic devices into a single power strip and then simply switching off the power strip when you leave the room.

Get an Energy Audit

Many states offer free or reduced-cost energy audits. If your state offers these audits, please take advantage of them. An energy audit is the first and often easiest way to begin conserving energy and saving money. The audit will reveal opportunities for reducing wasted energy and boosting energy efficiency. You'll find out exactly where your home or building is leaking heat in winter and losing cool air in the summer, which appliances and devices are costing you the most cash, and how to become a smarter consumer of energy in all of its many forms.

Use DSIRE

The Database of State Incentives for Renewable and Efficiency (DSIRE)[6] is a comprehensive database of incentives and policies for energy efficiency and renewable energy. DSIRE itself is a project of North Carolina Clean Energy Technology Center[7] at North Carolina State University. I cannot overstate the importance and value of DSIRE. It is my go-to resource, and it should be yours, too.

It's easy to use. Just go to the website (www.dsireusa.org) and follow the prompts to find policies and incentives in your area. You will be amazed at how many programs and policies already exist. You can tap into many of these programs for financial incentives that will add immediate value to your energy efficiency or renewable energy project.

For example, you can enter your ZIP code on the DSIRE website and see a list of incentives and programs available in your area. I urge you to try this now. Type in your ZIP code and you will see a list of available grants, loans, rebates, personal tax credits, corporate tax credits, sales tax credits, solar renewable energy credits, property tax incentives, corporate depreciation programs, appliance and equipment energy standards, corporate tax exemptions, financing, energy analysis, and training options.

I will explore the topic of economic incentives more thoroughly in Chapter 9 of this book. Meantime, visit the DSIRE website now and check out the available programs in your area. You will be pleasantly surprised to discover how many ways there are to earn tangible rewards for reducing your energy use.

Aim for Net-Zero Energy

Home and buildings account for nearly 40 percent of all the energy consumed in the United States.[8] In raw numbers, that translates into 40 quadrillion Btu (quads) of energy per year—a frightening amount by any reasonable measure. That's the bad news.

But here's the good news: Homes and buildings are easy targets for energy-efficiency projects. It doesn't take a huge investment of time or money to boost the energy efficiency of an existing home or building. New homes and buildings can be constructed to meet net-zero energy standards fairly easily. Net-zero energy simply means that your home or building returns as much energy to the grid as it takes. Talk to your architect or contractor about meeting or surpassing net-zero energy standards before you build.

Reducing wasted energy and raising energy efficiency don't have to be Herculean tasks. I've been surprised at how easy it can be to achieve higher levels of energy efficiency without breaking a sweat or breaking the bank. All it takes is the right mindset, a little knowledge, and a modest effort to have a positive impact on the environment that will last for decades, and possibly even for centuries, into the future. When I save energy, I feel as though I'm leaving a precious a gift for all of my generation's grandchildren and great-grandchildren.

When people find out that I'm an energy expert, they usually ask me for tips on saving energy. Here are some of my all-time favorites:

- Put covers on all pots when you are cooking to save heat.
- Use the appropriate size pan when cooking.
- Compost your food waste.
- Raise your air conditioning two degrees.
- Lower your heat two degrees.
- Put motion sensors on the lights you use most often so they turn themselves off when you leave the area. The lights in your hallways, for example, should have motion sensors.
- Do not let your car idle.
- Return bottles to the store instead of putting them in your single-stream recycling bin. Or donate them to a charitable organization.[9]

Endnotes

1. https://www.energy.gov/energysaver/home-heating-systems
/furnaces-and-boilers

2. https://www.energy.gov/eere/buildings/appliance-and-equipment
-standards-program

3. https://www.regulations.doe.gov/eecompass

4. https://www.eversource.com/content/ct-c/residential/save-money
-energy/explore-alternatives/electric-vehicles/ev-charger
-demand-response

5. https://native.eco/2017/11/phantom-load-how-unplugging
-can-save-you-100-or-more/

6. https://www.dsireusa.org/

7. https://nccleantech.ncsu.edu/

8. https://www1.eere.energy.gov/buildings/publications/pdfs
/corporate/bt_stateindustry.pdf

9. https://lifehacker.com/dont-crush-cans-before-recycling-them
-1833374490; https://justbeerapp.com/article/beer-cans-vs-bottles
-whats-better-why; https://homeguides.sfgate.com/energy-recycle
-glass-bottles-vs-aluminum-cans-vs-plastic-79276.html

Chapter 6

Focus on What's Doable

O ver the course of my career as an energy consultant, I've noticed that the most successful projects are often the ones initiated by the owners or operators of a business or by the leaders of a community-based organization. Why do these individuals succeed while others fail?

Here's what I have observed: An energy project is more likely to succeed if its champion has hands-on operational knowledge of the business or organization and has the clout to keep the project moving forward, even when surprises and setbacks are encountered along the way. If you can deal with disappointments and weather the storm, you are much more likely to succeed than if you throw in the towel at the first sign of difficulty.

Another characteristic I noticed was a fascination with energy. Most of the owners and executives I work with are genuinely interested in energy. They like the idea of being smart leaders and good stewards of our shared environment. For them, energy efficiency isn't a passing fad—it's become a deeply embedded part of their lives, influencing every aspect of their worldview. They've become "energy believers."

In this chapter, I offer short profiles of successful energy projects and the people who led them. After you've read these profiles, you'll understand why I stress the importance of focusing on what's doable, practical, and affordable.

The Solar Brewery

Rob Kaye didn't expect to open a brewery in his sixties. "I didn't even like beer," he recalls somewhat sheepishly. His attitude to beer changed after a visit to Austria. "My daughter was studying in Salzburg and we decided to take a family holiday there. We all went to Augustiner Bräu, a local brewery and beer hall. My son Dave suggested this would be the place to try the beer. It was amazing. That's when I became a fan."

When the family was back home, Rob's son made another suggestion. "He said, 'Dad, let's open a brewery.' I thought about it and said, 'Maybe in a couple of years.' Then I looked around and saw how many breweries were opening up. Clearly, there was a market for craft beer. And I knew instinctively that if we didn't act quickly, we would miss our opportunity to gain a position in the market."

In 2015, Rob had purchased an industrial building in Ridgefield, Connecticut, for his fencing company. In 2017, Rob and Dave launched Nod Hill Brewery in the front part of the building, reserving the back part for the fencing business.

People have brewed beer for millennia. Human culture has evolved, yet the basics of brewing have remained remarkably constant since the dawn of recorded history. "You take malt and grind it up. Then you put the ground-up malt in a mash tun and add hot water. You take the resulting mash and put in another tun, where you separate the liquid from the grain," Rob explains. "Next you take the liquid and boil it in the kettle. Then you add hops for flavor. Then you add yeast and let it ferment. You filter it and you cool it down, and then you set it aside to mature for a while. There are other steps, but that's basically the process."

Brewing is a lot like baking. There's a wonderful aroma of yeast and grain, similar to a bakery early in the morning. When I talk with Rob and his brewers, I can imagine our ancestors brewing beer thousands of years ago, stoking wood or charcoal fires to keep the vats of mash boiling.

Fast forward back to the twenty-first century: Brewing is still an energy-intensive process. The main difference is that modern brewers use electricity instead of wood for power.

"Pretty much every part of the brewing process requires electricity," Rob says. "Solar power was always in the back of my mind, and this felt like a perfect time to look into it." When he purchased the building, he had been told by an inspector that its 32,000-square-feet roof was "in pretty good shape." But a later and more thorough inspection revealed that the roof wasn't strong enough to support the weight of an industrial-strength array of solar panels over an expected life span of twenty-five years. That meant Rob had to fix the roof, "which was an unexpected expense," he observes matter-of-factly.

And there were other bumps in the road. An existing loan from the US Small Business Administration had to be paid off in order to obtain a loan from the Connecticut Green Bank to cover the cost of the solar panels. Delays in financing led to other delays. Part of the installation work was delayed because of winter, leading to yet additional delays.

It cost about $250,000 to fix the roof and about $750,000 to install the solar array. On April 4, 2019, Nod Hill Brewery became fully solar powered. A 287 kW photovoltaic solar array now offsets all of the brewery's electrical use and pushes at least 5,618 kWh per year back into the power grid. Rob considers the project a good investment.

"The solar panels, in combination with some other improvements, doubled the value of the building. When you look at all the numbers, including tax credits and accelerated depreciation, we came out ahead. Frankly, I am amazed at how much money we will save over the long term," Rob says. "Most important, however, is that we have met our own sustainability goals. We are the only 100% solar-powered brewery in the state of Connecticut. And that's good for our business. People love that we are doing this."

According to performance monitoring data posted on the SolarEdge website, the brewery has reduced its carbon emissions by 326,076 pounds, the equivalent of planting 8,213 trees.

From my perspective, Rob is a great role model. He's a small-town entrepreneur with a conscience who wants to earn a reasonable return on his investment and give back to the community that supports his business. To me, people like Rob are the backbone of a new environmental movement that blends practical business wisdom and real-world experience with genuine heartfelt concern for our planet's future.

Making Pasta and Conserving Energy

Woman-owned and family-operated, Carla's Pasta looks more like a NASA laboratory than a food factory. Everything in the place is spotless and shining. When I walk around Carla's, I feel like I'm a time traveler visiting a gleaming utopian version of the future.

The facility doesn't just look incredibly clean—it is! There are more than 21,000 food processing plants in the United States, but Carla's Pasta is the only one that meets the world's highest hygiene standard for ready-to-eat filled pasta. When I eat Carla's Pasta, I know that I'm eating one of the safest food products on the market.

Here are fascinating snippets from the company's promotional video:

> Our facility has three separate hygiene sectors, designed to protect pathogens from entering food production areas . . . Our facility features strategically placed drains and sloping floors which eliminate standing water. Twenty-one-inch stainless steel concrete-filled baseboards and one-quarter-inch-thick antimicrobial coated floors prevent cracks and chips, which eliminates bacterial harborage points.

> The use of multi-zone stainless steel air ducts in high hygiene areas creates positive air pressure to prevent outside air from entering, minimizing any risk of foreign airborne contaminants. HEPA filtration removes foreign matter from the air. Ultraviolet lighting disinfects the air after it has passed through the filters.

> Underneath the facility, an isolated multi-zone draining system carries wastewater away from each sector

independently, so the plant is never at risk for contamination from wastewater, if a backup were ever to occur. Additionally, the drain pipes themselves are bound together, using a process called electrofusion, which provides a seamless welded seal between sections of pipe, reducing the opportunity for pathogens to propagate.

An environmental monitoring program is strictly enforced throughout the building to seek out any traces of pathogens.

Enormous amounts of power are required for maintaining those ultra-high levels of hygiene. When Carla's Pasta hired our firm to audit its energy use, we felt the full weight of responsibility for making sure that none of our recommendations would compromise the safety or quality of its products.

Like good detectives, we began by looking at small and seemingly inconsequential details. We put the company's tax bills under a magnifying glass and we looked carefully at every item related to energy. We knew that many companies are exempt from certain taxes on gas and electricity, yet it's not uncommon to discover tax charges levied on energy fees that are not supposed to be taxed.

Finding those kinds of charges is like finding money in your pocket. You would be surprised how often it happens, which is why companies need to look carefully at their energy bills.

We also looked at all the facility's backup systems. A food processing plant such as Carla's Pasta has redundant systems to make sure its perishable products won't be lost if the power fails. Similar to many manufacturing plants, Carla's had a fuel cell that was designed to provide energy in the event of a power failure. We tested the fuel cell and discovered that it wasn't working properly. Worse yet, the fuel cell was drawing unnecessary power.

The third strike against the fuel cell was that it didn't have a "black start" capability, which means that if there had been a widespread power failure, the fuel cell would have been useless because it wouldn't have had the power to start it up.

To make a long story short, we had the fuel cell replaced, solving three significant problems in one swoop. By the way, fuel cells are expensive. Some of them cost millions of dollars. Fuel cell problems don't seem sexy, but they can be consequential, especially if your company cannot afford to go without power for several hours or days.

Finding Efficiencies in Steelmaking

Ulbrich Stainless Steels & Special Metals is a global producer of specialized industrial materials used in high-durability products such as fire extinguishers, mobile phones, solar panels, precision surgical instruments, and spacecraft. "Every LEM (lunar excursion module) on the moon has three hundred pounds of our metal in it," says Chris Ulbrich, the company's chairman and chief executive officer. "Our metals can withstand the freezing cold of space and the extreme heat of rocket engines."

Founded by Chris's grandfather in 1924, the company began as a scrap metal reseller in Wallingford, Connecticut. Its initial manufactured product was cutlery, and during World War II, the company won a contract to supply stainless steel knives for the US Army's mess kits. The contract enabled the company to purchase its first rolling mill and led to Ulbrich's transformation from a utensils-based manufacturer to a custom stainless steel strip operation in the post–World War II era. The company is now in its fourth generation of family management.

In addition to stainless steel, Ulbrich produces 160 different alloys, including nickel and nickel alloys, cobalt alloys, titanium and titanium alloys, and bi-metals such as silver-plated copper-clad aluminum and silver-plated copper-clad steel. Ulbrich's metals are produced in a variety of forms, including precision strip and foil, fine and flat wire, shaped wire, ribbon wire, sheet, and plate.

Manufacturing these kinds of specialty products requires deep knowledge of metallurgy and decades of experience. It also requires vast amounts of energy.

"We probably spend close to $1.8 million a year on electricity," says Chris. "Reducing that cost by a fraction every year really adds up to major savings over a ten-year period." Several years ago, the company decided to convert its mills from DC (direct current) to AC (alternating current).

The new AC machinery is quieter than DC, easier to repair, and uses less power. The company also made less dramatic changes, such as swapping its old sodium lights for modern LEDs (light emitting diodes). Each of the changes reduced the need for power and lowered the company's operating costs. "It's exciting to know that we're saving real money and helping the environment at the same time," Chris says.

The energy-efficiency project we conceived for one of Ulbrich's manufacturing facilities, a 44,000-square-foot specialty metal mill in Wallingford, Connecticut, shows the benefits of taking the time to fully understand the customer's processes and develop projects that make sense for each customer. As I've mentioned, there is no one-size-fits-all solution. Each situation is different and each customer requires a tailored solution that is practical, flexible, and context-specific. I wish there were shortcuts in this line of work, but there aren't.

For the metal mill in Wallingford, Ulbrich replaced an existing DC motor-and-drive system with an AC system that incorporated state-of-the-art controls and variable frequency drives (VFDs). To prove the changes were delivering greater efficiency and energy conservation, we added real-time recorders to collect baseline data on electrical consumption. Armed with the data, we could show before and after levels of efficiency and conservation.

The gross cost of the project was $770,000. The company will receive a $250,000 incentive from the local utility company, lowering its net cost to $520,000 and shortening the ROI time. The project reduced energy use at the facility by 1,203,000 kWh annually and 355 kW annually, which is roughly equivalent to saving 95,132 gallons of gasoline.

Understanding the process for incentives has made a tangible difference, says Chris. "We have earned more than $1.4 million over the past seven years in incentive dollars for electric and gas capital projects."

195 Church Street

Eighteen stories tall and situated in a prominent location in downtown New Haven, 195 Church Street is a quintessential "trophy" building, according to Chris Vigilante. Chris is the chief operating officer at Northside Development Company, where he manages the firm's day-to-day financial operations. He's also involved in planning, forecasting, and government approvals. Chris is a seasoned developer with a keen eye for value and an intuitive sense of market dynamics.

The 244,528-square-foot office building was put up for sale by its previous owner in 2015. "The owner was a bank, and it was very particular about who would own the property. If you wanted to be considered as a buyer, you had to make a bid and do a presentation, which is highly unusual in this business. We had to explain why we were the best buyer," Chris says.

That's when Chris contacted my firm. We quickly discovered the owner was paying $1.2 million per year for electricity, and we had a gut feeling we could reduce that amount substantially.

"The building dates back to 1974. It had single-pane glass and electric heat. It seems crazy today, but you have to remember that energy costs were much lower back then," Chris says.

We helped Chris prepare a detailed presentation that earned the owner's confidence and led to his firm winning the bid. Our collaboration with Chris is a great example of a modest-size project that boosts energy efficiency and delivers a healthy return on the customer's investment. Here's a brief recap of our work at 195 Church Street.

Initially, we performed an ASHRAE Level I audit. Based on the audit and our findings, we recommended a Phase 1 LED lighting upgrade and window insert project to increase the energy efficiency of the building.

Moreover, both projects could be accomplished with the least possible disruption to the building's tenants. The window inserts improved the building's efficiency level from a U-value of 1.03 to a U-value of .37. (U-values describe how well or how poorly doors and windows provide insulation; the lower the U-value, the better the insulation.) We converted all lighting to LED with plug-and-play LED tubes. We chose to disable (instead of replace) the ballast in the fixtures, which sped up the work and minimized disruptions.

The cost of the lighting was $253,042 and the cost of the window inserts was $1,539,802. Gross cost of project was $1,792,844. In terms of achieving efficiency, the results were impressive: The new lighting saved 674,290 kWh per year and the window inserts saved 773,404 kWh per year, reducing the building's annual energy use by a total of 1,447,694 kWh. That's the rough equivalent of saving 26,367 trees.

Here's another benefit to keep in mind: Because the projects qualified for incentives from the utilities, the building's owners received $579,078, reducing the net cost of the projects to $1,213,766.

Along the way, we kept a sharp watch on energy markets so we could help Chris find the most economical sources for electricity. Energy is similar to other commodities—its price fluctuates, depending on supply and demand.

The overall lesson is that energy-efficiency projects don't have to be financial burdens. If you do them correctly, you will recover your investment within a reasonable time frame, earn additional money through annualized cost savings, and reduce your carbon emissions.

"We took a building that had an annual electric bill of about $1.2 million and we crunched those electricity costs down to between $750,000 and $800,000. That's a huge difference. When you lower a building's operating costs, it becomes more valuable," Chris says. "In this case of this building, the increase in market value is significant."

Chapter 7

The Power of Local Action

Energy conservation and energy efficiency are truly global issues, but I'm a firm believer in finding local solutions for even the largest problems. "Think globally, act locally" is more than a cliché; it captures the reality of human nature. We don't like to have solutions imposed on us by largely invisible authorities. We're more likely to adopt homegrown practices that appeal to our innate sense of virtue. In our hearts, most of us are kind and generous. When given the opportunity, we will act in the common interest and do the right thing.

In this chapter, I share stories of people who joined the battle for energy efficiency and who made a difference. Ideally, these stories will inspire you and embolden you to become an active participant in the fight to reduce our collective carbon footprint and preserve the world.

A Virtuous Circle

Ed Boman is the assistant director of public works in the Town of Fairfield, Connecticut. If you were casting a movie, Ed would be the perfect choice to play the pragmatic New Englander who's spent most of his adult life working in town government. He definitely looks and sounds like a guy who knows his way around a backhoe and understands the intricacies of municipal drainage systems.

Ed is also a driving force in Fairfield's remarkably steady march toward a clean energy future. "Ed Boman is absolutely tenacious," says Scott Thompson of the Sustainable Fairfield Task Force. "He knows every source of funding out there and he knows the rules for each one. He puts it all together and gets projects done like no one else I've ever met. He is truly relentless in his pursuit of energy efficiency."

Fairfield is consistently ranked a leader in sustainability, thanks in large part to the high level of cooperation between the town and local volunteer groups such as the task force, the Earth Day Committee, the Forest Committee, and the Land Acquisition Commission. These grassroots efforts influence state lawmakers, who then pass legislation promoting sustainable energy practices. "After the laws are passed, it's up to local folks to implement them," Scott explains. "It's like a feedback loop, between the state and the local communities."

I agree with Scott's description of the process as a feedback loop. I also see it as an example of a virtuous circle in which one good deed leads to another, promoting a continuous series of small steps that add up significantly over time. "Collectively, the town saves about $3 million annually on its energy bills," Scott says. "That's measurable success. If people don't perceive the benefits, these projects die."

Scott shared the task force's approach and the key elements of success they identified:

- Leverage private sector and incentives
- Develop favorable PPA templates to minimize town risk
- Focus on economic arguments to gain approvals
- Truly engage stakeholders: listen and respond
- Share and promote success

Ed is equally adamant about the need for achieving tangible results from energy-efficiency projects. "The taxpayers have to see the cost savings. They have to see that you're reducing air pollution and improving public health," Ed says. "You've got to show them this isn't pie-in-the-sky stuff."

The town has two ongoing microgrid projects, one in the downtown commercial district and one at a former landfill at the town's water pollution control facility. The microgrids will ensure that essential town services such as police, fire, communications, and wastewater treatment can operate during power outages.

Highlights of Fairfield Microgrid Projects

Microgrid 1: Public Safety
- 300 kW natural gas generator; 60 kW CHP • 47 kW solar PV and efficiency measures • Control and distribution system, on-grid, and island modes • $1.1 million grant from CTDEEP's microgrid pilot program, $130k local share—serves police headquarters, fire headquarters, emergency communications, cell phone towers, and homeless shelter

---

Microgrid 2: Public Health

■ $2,850,000 grant received, no local share, under construction • 1.3 MW PV installed on former landfill • PV systems installed on fire training center, conservation garage, and animal control center—1,000,000 kwh/yr in energy conservations measures completed • 4,000,000 kwh/yr fuel cell in operation—70kw CHP generator using waste methane planned • goal net-zero energy at the water pollution control facility

---

One of the benefits of microgrids is that they can be powered by traditional sources of energy, nontraditional sources of energy, or by combinations of both, which makes them highly attractive sources of alternative power for neighborhoods, communities, college campuses, and office parks.

The town installed a solar array at the old landfill and a fuel cell to generate power and offset the high costs of operating the wastewater treatment plant, which treats nine million gallons of wastewater on an average day and twenty-five million gallons per day during heavy rainstorms.

Ed would like to see the wastewater plant and adjacent town buildings fully powered by renewable energy sources in the next couple of years. "Today, we use naturally generated methane to heat the building during the winter, but in the summer, the methane is vented," Ed explains. "If we convert to cogen [cogenerated power], we can burn the methane to produce electricity and heat. Then the buildings will be fully independent of outside power sources. That's our goal."

If Fairfield's energy plans are realized, the town will reduce electricity use by 20 percent, increase use of clean energy by 20 to 75 percent, reduce carbon emissions by 50 percent, and reduce town building maintenance costs by 20 percent.

I asked Ed how Fairfield had been able to move forward on a steady pace with its energy-efficiency projects. His reply speaks volumes: "We started early and kept going. Once you achieve some success, people accept it as normal. We use solar panels on rooftops and in parking lots. Almost every school in town generates solar energy. Parents are conscious of the health benefits and they know we're saving money. It gets to be a no-brainer after a while. People understand that it's a continuous process. You're not going to just do it once; you're always looking for improvements."

I really admire Ed's hands-on approach to energy efficiency. In many ways, he is emblematic of the global movement away from fossil fuels and toward cleaner sources of energy that are better for the environment. He is strong in his beliefs and yet realistic. He clearly is a fan of clean energy, and yet he is also aware of its complexities.

"You don't want to generate more green power than you can use," he says. "In Connecticut, when you collect more solar than you can use, it goes into a bank. In the wintertime, when there's less sun, you can use the energy you put in the bank. If you have leftover power at the end of the year, the utility company will buy it back at 4 cents per kWh."

The problem is that it costs 7 to 11 cents per kWh to generate solar power, which means you can't just blithely go ahead and switch to solar without considering the long-term financial consequences. In other words, you need a plan, and your plan has to take all the variables into account.

Everything Is Local

I've had several long and wonderful conversations with Mark Scully and Bernie Pelletier of People's Action for Clean Energy (PACE), an organization whose mission is transitioning Connecticut to clean energy through grassroots education and advocacy.[1]

Mark is the president of PACE and Bernie is the group's vice president. Both are retired insurance industry executives, with deep experience in actuarial science. These guys are all about data, and when they talk about environmental risks from CO_2, they aren't exaggerating.

PACE was formed in 1973, and it has a long track record of effective organizing. If you're interested in becoming part of the clean energy movement on the local level, I strongly urge you to visit the PACE website (https://pacecleanenergy .org/) and familiarize yourself with their resources. Here are selections (quoted with permission) from their comprehensive list of activities for building a project team and encouraging grassroots community engagement:

Getting Started: Project Team[2]

The first step to undertaking a project of this scope is to build a project team. Transitioning to clean energy will impact every aspect of town life, so you will want the team to include broad representation. If your town already has a Clean Energy Task Force or Commission, you might choose to work through this group. If not, you might consider forming one, as it can help your team be more effective.

Before jumping into the technical details, it is wise to establish an initial project vision, scope, high-level goals, and approach.

Build a Project Team

Because this transition will touch every community member the team should be a cross section of the community members. It will require business owners, key municipal staff, local grassroots organizations, and large sector representatives. The idea is to assemble a group that is diverse enough to represent your community and engaged enough to help you get things done after planning. Having diverse representation from across your community is necessary to develop a credible and actionable plan. Additionally, a varied group of planning team members may be able to help you leverage broader resources to support implementation.

In forming your team, you might want to consider representation from the following groups:

- *Civic leaders*
- *Neighborhood groups*
- *Business groups (e.g., Chamber of Commerce)*
- *Service organizations (e.g. Rotary, Lions)*
- *Environmental organizations*
- *Workforce and educational providers*
- *Energy-efficiency contractors*
- *Green-building guilds or groups*

- *Faith-based organizations*
- *Municipal staff*
  - *Public Works*
  - *Economic development*
  - *Land use planning*
  - *Environmental staff*
- *Larger sources of emissions*
  - *Hospitals*
  - *University and community colleges*
  - *K–12 energy managers*
  - *Other major employers*
- *Individuals with relevant expertise*
  - *Energy policy, advocacy or technical experts*
  - *Regional and state partners that you may already work with*

Form a Clean Energy Task Force/Commission

Across the country, clean energy task forces and commissions have proven to be effective groups in promoting the transition to clean energy. These entities speak with the authority of having been commissioned by the town authorities to address energy issues. As such, their recommendations and plans have greater authority and impact than those from other groups.

Establish Initial Project Vision, Scope, High-Level Goals, and Approach

For a project as bold and wide-ranging as the transition to renewable energy, it is essential for the team to share a common understanding of the basic project features.

Clearly, many of these features will evolve as the project progresses, but it is important to take time up front to establish a common view of a few core areas, such as Vision, Scope, High-Level Goals, and Approach. (For example, your Vision will be a "clearly articulated, transparent, and shared vision of your community's energy future sets the direction for subsequent decisions about focus areas, goals, and strategies for achieving those goals." Your Approach might include, "How often will your team meet? Are you planning a larger workshop to determine the vision, scope, and goals? What partners do you plan to engage? Will you conduct media outreach?")

Getting Started: Energy Plan[3]

If you haven't done so already, start by discussing and agreeing upon a vision for your community's energy future. What are your high-level goals and interim milestones? What will be the scope of your vision (e.g., residents, businesses, municipality, schools)?

Next, assess the resources available to you. Does your town have a prior plan you can build on? Is the municipality able to provide assistance such as staff time, publication tools, work space? Are you able to partner with local educational institutions or other organizations? Are there individuals in your town with particular skills or expertise that you might recruit to help? Do you have funding to engage consultants or graphic designers?

Peruse a range of plans from other towns. You will find a rich diversity of styles and content. What features, language, charts, or images appeal to you? [Don't be shy about reaching out to that town—or to PACE—for assistance or permission to use their images or other features.]

Finally, decide on the style, scope, and organization of your plan. Is there a particular plan or template you want to start with, or will you start from scratch?

Checklist

If you haven't already done so, carry out a Baseline Energy Assessment.[4] It will provide some quantitative analysis, charts, and direction for the plan.

Divvy up the work and create your plan. You will want to thoroughly discuss your concrete actions amongst your team. While it may not be possible to achieve unanimity, aim for a consensus on these action steps.

Once you have a fairly complete draft of the plan, set about engaging the community. The more stakeholders understand the plan, and feel they had a chance to provide input, the more credibility it will have, and the more likely you will be able to implement it. Key stakeholders to engage include:

- *Town officials (e.g., First Selectmen, Mayor, Town Manager, Director of Public Works, Energy Manager)*
- *Board of Education*
- *Schools, parent-teacher organizations*
- *Residents*
- *Neighborhood organizations*
- *Businesses, business groups*
- *Religious organizations*

After revising the plan based on input from the community, ask your town officials (i.e., Town Council, Board of

Selectmen) to approve it. An official vote and/or resolution of support will be invaluable as you implement the plan.

Celebrate and publicize its passage! Get an article in the local paper. Go on local television. Create banners, buttons, and so on.

Revisit your plan annually. It should not need a complete rewrite, but you need to update your one-year and five-year plans (or whatever time horizon you use).

Getting Started: Community Engagement[5]

If you haven't done so already, make sure all key stakeholders have seen and provided input into your energy plan. Discussions with stakeholder groups will not only improve the plan, but they will [also] uncover diverse and original ways to carry it out. And, along the way, you will identify champions to carry different initiatives forward.

Checklist

- *Identify key stakeholders in your community and determine the best way to engage each of them.*
- *As a plan is developed, intermediate approvals are useful. For example, a Clean Energy Task Force approval is a valuable stepping stone to larger community adoption.*
- *After revising the plan based on input from the community, ask your town officials (i.e., Town Council, Board of Selectmen) to approve it. An official vote and/or resolution of support will be invaluable as you implement the plan.*
- *Reach out to Sierra Club Connecticut and consider joining their Ready for 100 Campaign.*

- *Carry out your own combination of activities (e.g., workshops, energy fairs, surveys, social networking, public displays, informational campaigns).*
- *Conduct each activity through the equity lens.*

This list is merely a portion of the excellent guidance provided by the PACE team. I recommend taking a deep dive into their website and taking full advantage of the excellent work they've already done. In addition to links to other towns with energy task forces or commissions, you will also find a customizable template[6] for creating an energy plan for your town or community. I find resources such as these to be absolutely essential for reducing your workload substantially and improving your chances for success.

Strong Legal Framework Is Essential

The Pacific Northwest is home to many of the nation's major hydroelectric plants. It also has easy access to electricity generated by coal-burning plants in Montana, Wyoming, and Utah.

It seems odd that a region blessed with cheap power would become a model of energy efficiency. Despite an abundance of inexpensive energy sources, the Pacific Northwest is a trailblazer in power economics.

The region's pioneering journey toward energy efficiency began in the nineteenth century, when early settlers realized they could use the flowing currents of local rivers to power their mills. In 1885, George Fitch built the region's first hydroelectric generator near the Spokane River.

He installed a small dynamo, powered by the river, in the basement of a flour mill and sent electricity to a dozen arc lights a short distance away. Four years later, in 1889, the first long-distance transmission of electricity in the Northwest began in Portland, where a direct-current line was built from a small hydropower plant at Willamette Falls to light street lights downtown, a distance of about 13 miles.[7]

The success of Fitch's arc dynamo inspired a legion of copycats. Soon there were "run-of-river" generators and hydroelectric dams across the Northwest. In retrospect, it makes perfect sense. The combination of frontier ingenuity and the vast waters of the Columbia River Basin spawned a robust economy based on hydroelectricity.

As a New Englander, it's hard for me to imagine the sheer size of the Columbia River Basin. It encompasses portions of Washington, Oregon, Idaho, Montana, Wyoming, Utah, Nevada, and British Columbia. The Columbia River Basin is larger than the nation of France!

During the 1930s, large-scale hydroelectric projects such as the Grand Coulee Dam transformed both the regional and national economies. The lasting impacts of these projects are incalculable. As of today, the Pacific Northwest region depends on hydropower for roughly 50 percent of its electrical needs. This power is also widely shared: About 40 percent of all the hydropower used in the United States originates in the Columbia River Basin system.[8]

But let's take a step back and revisit a critical moment in the energy history of the Pacific Northwest. By the mid-1960s, virtually all of the region's electricity was generated by hydropower. Then a confluence of events forced the people of the Pacific Northwest to rethink the future of their energy sources.

First, the region's growing population and expanding economy required more energy. At the same time, however, the region simply ran out of places to build new hydroelectric dams. Next, a natural meteorological phenomenon called the Pacific Decadal Oscillation[9] reduced the flow of water in the Columbia River Basin. The oil embargoes of the 1970s drove up energy prices, ending a long period of inexpensive and readily available power.

Facing a growth in demand and limited new sources of hydropower, the region shored up its energy needs with inexpensive electricity from coal-fired generators in the intermountain states and the development of nuclear power. But a general sense of uneasiness over nuclear energy and rising awareness of coal's harmful impact on the environment led many people in the region to seek alternatives that were less risky and more friendly to the natural landscape. By the late 1970s, it had become apparent that new sources of energy were needed.

This was the moment at which energy efficiency began to emerge as a serious long-term strategy. "We saw a cloud on the horizon," recalls Angus Duncan, who served on the Northwest Power and Conservation Council, a four-state organization authorized by Congress to "develop, with broad citizen participation, a regional power plan to ensure an adequate, efficient, economical, and reliable power supply, along with a program to protect and enhance fish and wildlife affected by hydropower dams in the basin."[10]

The looming cloud they saw was climate change. "We began thinking about how we would have to change the way we use energy to cope with that," Angus remembers. The council's efforts to develop exceptionally strong regional policies programs for energy efficiency also positioned the Northwest to move forward on climate change mitigation strategies.

Thanks largely to those policies and programs, the Pacific Northwest has become a leader in the energy-efficiency movement. Efficiency is now the region's second-largest energy resource after hydropower. The strong focus on efficiency has made it possible for the region to build fewer power plants. According to statistics from the council's Regional Technical Forum, the region has met more than half its load growth with energy efficiency since 1978, resulting in these savings:

- More than 6,000 average megawatts saved, enough power for five Seattles
- $4 billion saved in lower electricity bills per year
- Carbon emissions reduced by 23.5 million tons per year
- Producing more with less energy compared to the national average

In hindsight, the region's decision to concentrate on energy efficiency seems like a no-brainer. But in the 1980s, when the Pacific Northwest was paying substantially less for energy than other parts of the nation, it took considerable foresight to pivot sharply and focus on efficiency.

"One of the things we wrote into the federal law setting this all up was that you have to treat energy efficiency as though it's a generating resource," Angus explains. "You have to think about efficiency as a tangible resource, not just as a frill or an extra."

From his perspective, greater efficiency translates directly into long-term savings because it is the equivalent of not having to build a new generating resource. "We've saved between two and three Grand Coulee Dams' worth of energy in the last 30 years. Which means we have *not* built fifteen to twenty additional coal or gas plants we otherwise would have had to build to meet our energy needs," Angus says. "It's been a real economic benefit because this is money we *didn't* have to spend on construction and operations."

One of the key lessons I learned from over the course of my conversations with Angus is the importance of a solid legal framework for guiding and informing the development of energy strategy.

The US Pacific Northwest Electric Power Planning and Conservation Act of 1980, more commonly known as the Northwest Power Act, has played an absolutely essential role in the creation and implementation of the region's energy-efficiency strategy. The act serves as map, compass, and rulebook for navigating successfully through the complexities of energy policy. At a high level, the act sets forth three bedrock principles:

- Energy efficiency must be regarded as equivalent to an energy resource.
- Energy efficiency must be prioritized over building new power plants.
- When new energy plans are considered, integrated resource planning techniques must be used to determine the least-cost option.

"If you want to build a new power plant, you have to do an analysis showing that it's the least-cost option," Angus explains. "Additionally, when you're calculating costs, you have to look not just at dollar costs, but at environmental costs and benefits as well. If you can put a dollar figure on them, you have to add them into your dollar calculation. Even if you can't put a dollar value to them, they still have to be stated and they have to be a part of the record of the decision process."

For many readers, that might sound overly wonky. Yet the strength of the Northwest Power Act is in its details. As a lawyer, I appreciate carefully written laws because they make life easier. The Northwest Power Act was largely written by people who live and work in the Pacific Northwest region. The act has stood the test of time and has enabled the region to pursue its goal of energy efficiency successfully since the 1980s. It's become a model for legislation worldwide, and it's worth studying.

Endnotes

1. The PACE group referenced in this chapter should not be confused with CPACE, an energy financing program.
2. https://pacecleanenergy.org/initial-project-organization
3. https://pacecleanenergy.org/energy-plan
4. https://pacecleanenergy.org/baseline-assessment
5. https://pacecleanenergy.org/community-engagement
6. https://pacecleanenergy.org/wp-content/uploads/2020/01 /2020_PACE_Energy_Plan_Template_v1.0.pptx

7. https://www.nwcouncil.org/reports/columbia-river-history/hydropower

8. https://app.nwcouncil.org/ext/storymaps/damguide/index.html

9. https://www.ncdc.noaa.gov/teleconnections/pdo/

10. https://www.nwcouncil.org/sites/default/files/eeonepager.pdf

Chapter 8

Conservation, Efficiency, and Generation

The most direct way of conserving a limited resource is by using less of it. Conservation isn't a new idea; even single-cell organisms such as amoebas and algae have mastered the essentials of conservation. Yet many people resist the simple notion of applying basic conservation techniques to reduce their use of energy.

What do microscopic life forms know that we don't? On some level, those tiny creatures apparently have a better understanding of how the world works than we do. For a variety of reasons, we have developed a warped perception of energy. We tend to see it as cheap and unlimited; in truth it is neither.

Inefficient use of energy really upsets me. I grew up poor, and I learned the value of frugality early in life. From my perspective, inefficiency is a form of unnecessary waste. To me, it feels like throwing away money. Using energy efficiently, however, is like putting money in the bank. That's why I spend the majority of my time helping people and companies use energy more efficiently.

Conservation and efficiency are two-thirds of the overall solution to our global energy problem. The remaining third is generation. We'll look at all three in this chapter. Here's an important takeaway based on my decades of experience: Your primary focus should be on reducing your overall energy needs through conservation and efficiency. I'm not saying that generation isn't important, but you'll achieve your energy goals sooner by prioritizing conservation and efficiency.

Inefficient Systems Are Everywhere

Energy inefficiency is rampant and ubiquitous. But there is an upside: Because inefficiency is such a common problem, there's no shortage of practical strategies for dealing with it. Every inefficient machine, device, or system presents a golden opportunity for improving efficiency and saving energy.

Look into any commercial or industrial building and you will find legions of inefficiencies to conquer and vanquish. Typical culprits include windows, insulation, lighting, roofing, refrigerators, ovens, pumps, HVAC (heating, ventilation, and air conditioning), and control technologies such as thermostats and sensors.

Increasing the efficiency of existing energy systems and intentionally using less energy by practicing conservation will contribute significantly to reducing energy costs.

Building Codes and Energy Efficiency

Most people whom I speak with understand that reducing energy use and costs and slowing the pace of climate change are worthy goals. Very few of them, however, understand how to accomplish these goals. There's a disconnect between their good intentions and their ability to take positive action.

To be fair, this is not an uncommon situation. All of us have experienced the predicament of wanting to do something and yet not knowing how to do it. That's when you either give up or start looking for help. Fortunately for those of us who want to become more energy efficient and are looking for a guiding star, there is ASHRAE, "a global society advancing human well-being through sustainable technology for the built environment."[1]

ASHRAE's mission is "to serve humanity by advancing the arts and sciences of heating, ventilation, air conditioning, refrigeration, and their allied fields" through "research, standards writing, publishing, and continuing education." The organization has a long and venerable history:

> *ASHRAE was formed as the American Society of Heating, Refrigerating and Air-Conditioning Engineers by the merger in 1959 of American Society of Heating and Air-Conditioning Engineers (ASHAE) founded in 1894 and The American Society of Refrigerating Engineers (ASRE) founded in 1904.*[1]

ASHRAE's backstory is relevant because it demonstrates clearly that the pursuit of energy efficiency isn't a new trend or passing fad. I find it reassuring to know that people have been thinking seriously about energy efficiency since the days of Queen Victoria.

ASHRAE and the International Codes Council (ICC) develop the energy codes used in commercial and residential buildings across the United States. Many people are surprised to discover that private organizations such as ASHRAE and the ICC draft the codes, but that's the way it works here in the United States, which has no formal national energy or building codes.

Here's a quick overview of how the process works: ASHRAE develops a model code known as 90.1 for commercial buildings and the ICC develops a model code for both commercial and residential buildings called International Energy Conservation Code (IECC).

ASHRAE and the ICC update their code model every three years. The US Department of Energy (DOE) participates in drafting and reviewing the updated models. The DOE also provides technical assistance, helping states and cities adopt the updated model codes.

In the United States, states and local governments are free to use the model codes developed by ASHRAE and the ICC. Some jurisdictions adopt parts of the model codes and some develop their own codes.

New Buildings Institute (NBI) also plays an important role in developing model codes for improved energy performance in residential and commercial buildings. NBI works collaboratively with governments, utilities, energy efficiency advocates, and building professionals "to promote advanced design practices, innovative technologies, public policies, and programs that improve energy efficiency."[2]

NBI also helps local jurisdictions develop technical measures, evaluation techniques, and implementation plans necessary for enabling stronger codes. From my perspective, organizations such as NBI are essential to the widespread adoption of meaningful energy codes.

I had a fascinating conversation recently with Kim Cheslak, NBI's associate director of codes and policy. "Our vision is a transformed built environment that is carbon-free, sustainable, and energy efficient—and supports thriving economies that benefit people and the planet," Kim says. Translating that vision into reality, however, requires energy codes that are thoughtfully developed and carefully tested in the real world.

"Model energy codes are that final push to market transformation," she explains. "We test out early innovations through a voluntary process. We select the ones that have shown success and present them to organizations like the ICC. Our role is helping move those innovations that we know are working on the ground, in the vanguard cities and jurisdictions, and pulling them into national model codes that everyone can use."

After speaking with Kim and delving into the NBI website, I gained a deeper understanding of the code-creation process and its ultimate impact on the built environment. I also recommend visiting the DOE website and reading two excellent articles posted there: "Energy Codes 101: What Are They and What Is DOE's Role?"[3] and "How Are Building Energy Codes Developed?"[4]

One of the reasons I'm highlighting the efforts of organizations such as the ASHRAE, ICC, NBI, and the DOE is to demonstrate the nuances and complexities of the processes required to drive our economy toward greater energy efficiency. Developing and rolling out effective energy codes isn't easy work. Our nation's patchwork approach to energy policy poses incredible challenges. I'm all in favor of self-determination and limited government, but you should be aware that our federal system in the United States makes it very difficult to impose uniform energy-efficiency standards across the land.

Why does that matter? It matters because air pollution and carbon emissions don't respect state lines; toxic particulates and other pollutants are carried across state borders by wind currents. When fossil fuels are burned in Ohio, for example, the emissions usually travel east, affecting air quality in Pennsylvania, New York, Connecticut, and New Jersey. If you live east of a state with poor air quality, you and your family are breathing that state's pollution.

In a perfect world, all fifty states would agree on a common set of energy-efficiency standards. The idea of reaching a national consensus on energy isn't entirely far-fetched or fantastical. Every state has laws covering hundreds of crimes and misdemeanors, and many of those laws are virtually identical from state to state.

States also have extradition agreements that discourage felons from merely fleeing to another state after committing a crime. We have a long tradition of interstate cooperation in the United States, and I don't see any reason why a similar spirit of cooperation couldn't be extended to cover energy regulations.

Yes, it's inarguable that different communities have different energy needs and depend on different combinations of resources to generate power. Those differences must be acknowledged, and worked around. They shouldn't become insurmountable obstacles to progress. We cannot afford to slow down our efforts to conserve energy, use energy efficiently, and shift to cleaner and more sustainable sources of energy—too much is at stake.

Diving Deeper

Terms such as *energy conservation, energy efficiency, renewable energy, clean energy,* and *sustainable energy* are often used loosely in casual conversations, yet each has an important, specific meaning relevant to the larger picture. Here are three distinct areas in which understanding the terminology genuinely matters:

- Conservation
- Efficiency
- Generation

And now let's do a deeper dive into each of the three critical areas.

Conservation

Energy conservation refers to saving energy by using less of an energy-consuming device or machine. The device or machine is itself not necessarily more efficient. For example, if a company goes from using an inefficient incandescent lightbulb from fourteen hours per day to eight hours per day, they are conserving energy even if the lightbulb itself is inefficient. As a result, energy conservation generally entails using less output from the same energy source by installing sensors, software, and other devices that use existing technology to reduce energy use.

Light occupancy sensors are an example of energy conservation applied to buildings. Sensors installed next to light switches that detect room occupants will turn lights on; with lack of movement, the lights are turned off. Motion sensors and photo-sensors for outdoor lighting are also available. By turning off the lights when occupants are not present using occupancy sensors, we reduce energy waste that can result in a reduction in lighting energy consumption. According to the California Energy Commission, "Energy saving potential is highly dependent on baseline assumptions and operation, but values of 35% to 45% are typical."[5]

Lighting is one of many building components that consumes energy. Energy management and building management systems can be used to manage a whole building's energy use. These systems may provide a host of services, including tracking HVAC and lighting use, IT management, emissions information, energy optimization, and demand response (a voluntary program that compensates retail customers for reducing their electricity use on request during periods of high demand). Companies advertise 10 to 25 percent reductions in HVAC energy costs and 50 to 85 percent reductions in energy use using computers and network devices.[6]

Although the terms for energy management and building management systems are often used interchangeably, there are a few differences. Generally, building management systems have the ability to control energy-using equipment such as HVAC and lighting, whereas energy management systems may have only the ability to record use information. This distinction is key because energy reductions will be made more easily with a comprehensive system that adjusts and controls use. Either of these systems are set by the user specific to the requirements of your building and processing equipment, with alerts and alarms that are important to you.

Although energy and building management systems can effectively conserve energy, building energy systems also require ongoing preventive maintenance. Creating a maintenance plan is essential for getting the best ROI on any existing or new equipment or technology, and a company's higher management should engage in the creation of such a plan. HVAC and hot water heating, for example, need regular maintenance and constant commissioning to perform at peak efficiency. Overall, an energy/building management system that monitors and controls energy use and environmental air quality, and that detects system abnormalities and diagnoses common problems, can save a large amount of money in the end.

Smart meters, for instance, monitor energy use at frequent intervals and record energy use information. Smart meters generally help utility companies accurately predict energy use, and they enable customers to visualize energy use over time. With this increased awareness, customers can make more intelligent decisions and make energy use adjustments, with studies showing a 4 to 12 percent improvement in energy conservation using smart meters.[7]

VFD (variable frequency drive) or VAV (variable air volume) retrofits on HVAC systems are another very effective way to conserve energy and reduce energy consumption. A VFD is a device that changes the speed of an electric motor in an HVAC system by controlling the power frequency to the motor. VFDs can adjust to load requirements and enable fans to run at the speed that most adequately suits the situation. Energy savings vary from 35 to 50 percent over conventional constant speed applications. A VAV system produces air at a constant temperature, changing the airflow rate to ensure a comfortable temperature inside the building. This is in contrast to constant air volume (CAV) systems, which supply a constant airflow at a variable temperature.

The advantages of VAV systems over constant-volume systems include more precise temperature control, reduced compressor wear, and lower energy consumption by system fans. In large office buildings, this system is generally very efficient, and it only requires a small add-on to retrofit an existing HVAC system into a VAV system.

Efficiency

Here's an easy way to remember the difference between energy conservation and energy efficiency:

- Energy conservation is using less energy to run existing equipment.
- Energy efficiency is having equipment that requires less energy to run.

New technologies are improving energy efficiency at an exponential rate. The United States uses less oil now than it did in 1973, and we use less total energy than in 1999, even though our economy is more than 25 percent larger.[8] McKinsey and Company's research shows that investing in the energy efficiency of buildings can reduce energy consumption and save nearly $1.2 trillion in energy waste.[9]

Energy efficiency comes in many forms. Nearly every appliance and device that uses energy is more efficient today than in the past. Furthermore, building technologies have become very efficient. This is especially true for certain areas:

■ Lighting retrofit: New lighting technologies are extremely efficient. Replacing incandescent bulbs with compact fluorescent lamps (CFL) and light emitting diode (LED) lamps can lead to drastic savings. LEDs, in particular, can use up to 80 percent less energy, and CFLs use up to 75 percent less energy.

■ Appliances: Appliances such as refrigerators, washing machines, dryers, and dishwashers are much more efficient now than they were even ten years ago.

■ Technology: Computer and network technology, including data center equipment and servers have drastically lowered energy consumption. Modern technology uses a fraction of the energy of the earlier models.

■ Building insulation: Comparatively small upgrades such as wrapping, duct/air sealing, caulking, and weatherstripping can make an enormous difference and drastically change how much heat or cold air escapes the building.

■ Windows: Windows are much more efficient than they were in the past. Given the material and large surface area, windows are prime areas to improve energy inefficiency. Double-paned windows with argon or air between the panes are dramatically more efficient. Window inserts have become a solution for expensive historic windows that are difficult to update or large office buildings, where window replacements are costly and disruptive to the tenants, by increasing the efficiency of the current window area with little to no disruption, less cost, and no outdoor scaffolding.

- Roofs and siding: Roofs are especially important because
  an inefficient roof can make heating and cooling a
  building much more difficult. Roofs can have heat reflective material incorporated into them or they can be
  designed as a "cool roof." A cool roof is one that has
  been designed to reflect more sunlight and absorb less
  heat than a standard roof. Cool roofs can be made of a
  highly reflective type of paint, a sheet covering, or highly
  reflective tiles or shingles. Membrane roofing can also
  improve energy efficiency. A membrane roofing system,
  frequently made from synthetic rubber, is used on flat or
  nearly flat roofs to prevent leaks and to eliminate water
  buildup. Insulated siding can improve efficiency and
  increase the R-factor of the building. (R-values indicate
  the thermal resistance of insulation materials.)

- Chillers: The cooling process takes an immense amount
  of energy. Chillers use a large portion of overall HVAC
  energy consumption. Glycol chillers and other water-
  cooled energy-efficient chillers use less energy than older
  chlorofluorocarbon and air-cooled chillers. ASHRAE
  estimates 8 to 12 percent energy savings with a chiller
  replacement alone and a 38 percent peak energy demand
  reduction when combined with a lighting retrofit.

- Furnaces and boilers: Many highly efficient natural gas furnaces and boilers are available. With the price of oil today,
  many furnaces and boilers are being converted to run on
  natural gas. For a comparatively small cost, companies
  can benefit from cheaper natural gas. New high-efficiency
  natural gas furnaces and boilers can achieve 98 percent
  efficiency, compared to 70 to 80 percent efficiency for
  regular furnaces and boilers.

- Heat pumps: Heat pumps provide an efficient way to heat and cool water. Energy-efficient heat pumps electrically move heat from cool areas to warmer ones, resulting in colder cool areas and hotter warm areas. There are a variety of types of heat pumps:

  ◆ Air-source heat pumps: This heat pump transfers heat between a building and the outside. Some use similar technology but run on natural gas; these are known as absorption pumps.

  ◆ Mini-split heat pumps: This heat pump does the same as the air-source heat pump, but without a duct, and is generally used only for smaller applications.

  ◆ Geothermal heat pumps: These pumps use the relatively constant ground temperature to heat and cool buildings.

- Central air conditioners: Today's high efficiency air conditioners use 30 to 50 percent less energy than those made in the mid-1970s. However, they may use 20 to 40 percent less energy than those installed ten years ago as well.

Creating an energy-efficiency plan can seem like a daunting task, but it is actually enjoyable when you begin seeing results. Generally speaking, most energy-efficiency projects are relatively simple:

- Lighting retrofit including using daylight harvesting (self-adjusting, energy-efficient lighting system that harvests exterior daylight)
- Replacing appliances, office equipment, mechanicals, manufacturing equipment, and so on with more energy-efficient models

- Replacing windows or installing custom-made window inserts
- Installing lighting sensors, smart meters, and energy management systems
- Natural gas conversions for furnaces and boilers

These projects are great ways to start, and they apply to many of the current office buildings in the Northeast. Using energy-efficiency and conservation measures, businesses can easily reduce energy use by 30 percent, reducing costs by a similar percentage.[10] This percentage does not include monetary savings from energy generation or competitive energy pricing, which could provide additional savings as well.

Generation

Energy generation is the actual creation of energy on-site, usually in the form of electricity, from a variety of sources. Energy generation can be sustainable and create low carbon emissions. The following are some examples:

- Solar thermal collectors: There are two categories: concentrated solar thermal and concentrated solar power. When special panels, mirrors, or lenses concentrate light at a point, the point heats up rapidly. This thermal energy can then be used to create electricity through generators. The first installation occurred in 1910, and currently the Mohave Desert houses the largest solar thermal collector in the world.
- Solar photovoltaic (PV) systems: Sets of photovoltaic modules are what we've come to know as the classic

solar panel. These are the dark, glass arrays installed on roofs or on the ground. Photovoltaic modules work by directly converting sunlight into electricity. Large PV arrays work best on building roofs, and they can contribute a substantial amount of electricity. PV arrays are currently heavily subsidized, but the subsidies vary by location and whether the arrays will be applied to a residential or commercial building. The technology behind PV arrays has become more and more efficient, making these systems an increasingly viable option for energy generation.

- Wind energy: Small- and medium-sized wind turbines can make a significant contribution toward reducing electrical costs. The viability of wind turbines is contingent on location.

- Fuel cells: Fuel cells harvest chemical energy generally from the hydrogen atom. The process is extremely efficient, and the only by-products are heat and water. The size of the fuel cell can range from extremely small (one electronic device) to a utility power station. There are different types of fuel cells that vary based on the electrolyte they use. Different fuel cells are more appropriate for certain environmental conditions and loads.[11] One of the key characteristics of the fuel cell is that it produces both an electric load and a thermal (heat) load. This means that heat can be captured during the process of making electricity, which guarantees further reductions in energy use.

- CHP/cogeneration: This process is the concurrent production of electricity and heat from one fuel source. Generally speaking, CHP (combined heat and power) delivers electrical generation alongside waste-heat recovery, which can be used for heating and cooling. As a result, there is an electric load and a thermal load, as with fuel cells. There are two main types of cogen systems:

- ◆ Gas turbines or engines with a heat recovery unit: These units produce electricity and recover any heat from the original (combustion) process.
- ◆ Steam boiler with steam turbines: In these systems, electricity is made as the by-product of heat or steam.

■ Geothermal energy: Geothermal technology uses steam and hot water below the earth's surface to produce electricity. This technology is more popular along fault lines, such as in Iceland, but it can be used effectively in New England.

Many of these energy generation technologies are "clean" and "sustainable," producing only low levels of carbon or other toxic by-products from their processes and using natural, nondepleting resources as their source of energy:

■ Solar photovoltaic and solar thermal energy, which use the sun's natural ray
■ Wind energy, which uses wind as the energy source
■ Geothermal energy, which uses the earth's inner heat as the energy source

Other systems to consider:

■ Solar water heating systems: This system (active or passive) uses solar energy directly or indirectly by heating water. This is achieved by having water or another heat-transfer fluid run through a loop exposed to solar energy.

- Solar space heat systems: In this system (active or passive) solar energy directly or indirectly provides space heating. The technology is similar to solar water heat, but it can also include simpler techniques for using the sun, such as heating a corn glycol, which feeds a loop through the heating system in essence to preheat the energy source such as oil.

Endnotes

1. https://www.ashrae.org/about
2. https://newbuildings.org/about-nbi/
3. https://www.energy.gov/eere/buildings/articles/energy-codes
   -101-what-are-they-and-what-doe-s-role
4. https://www.energy.gov/eere/buildings/articles/how-are-building
   -energy-codes-developed
5. https://www.lightingdesignlab.com/resources/articles/articles
   -lighting-controls/introduction-occupancy-sensors
6. https://www.energystar.gov/ndex.cfm?c=power_mgt.pr_power
   _mgt_comm_packages
7. http://www.scientificamerican.com/article/do-smart-meters
   -mean-smart-electricity-use/
8. http://thinkprogress.org/climate/2013/10/17/2801231/world
   -energy-efficiency/
9. http://www.facilitiesnet.com/energyefficiency/article/McKinsey
   -Unlocking-Energy-Efficiency-Potential-in-Buildings-Could
   -Significantly-Bolster-Economy--11027
10. Ibid.
11. http://energy.gov/eere/fuelcells/types-fuel-cells

Chapter 9

Pricing Energy: It's Complicated

The power economy is a complicated beast, shrouded in lore and mystery. In this chapter, we will pull back the curtain and reveal the inner workings of the strangely convoluted ecosystem that supplies power to our homes and businesses. We will also look at some of the main drivers of price fluctuations in energy markets. These drivers include fracking, power plant decommissioning, and the steady rise of renewable energy.[1]

The net takeaway here is that energy markets aren't like the markets you studied in high school or college. I can't say with certainty what Adam Smith, author of *The Wealth of Nations*, would have thought about energy markets, but I can imagine him rolling his eyes at their tangled complexities and inconsistencies.

One of the first notions we need to discard is the idea that electricity is a natural resource. Electricity is a product.

It can be generated in a variety of ways, all of them requiring energy and equipment. Electricity is neither magical nor free.

Generating electricity involves costs and those costs have to be paid. In the United States, most electricity is produced through the burning of nonrenewable fossil fuels such as oil, coal, and natural gas. Electricity is also produced from sources such as running water (hydropower), sunlight (solar power), wind, ocean currents, thermal energy, and nuclear energy.

To get a sense of scale, here's a handy summary from the US Energy Information Administration (EIA) website:

> *In 2019, about 4,118 billion kilowatt-hours (kWh) (or about 4.12 trillion kWh) of electricity were generated at utility-scale electricity generation facilities in the United States. About 63% of this electricity generation was from fossil fuels—coal, natural gas, petroleum, and other gases. About 20% was from nuclear energy, and about 18% was from renewable energy sources . . . an additional 35 billion kWh of electricity generation was from small-scale solar photovoltaic systems in 2019.*[2]

Electricity Costs Are Variable and Inconsistent

Electricity costs are not consistent throughout the country; they vary considerably by region and by time of day. Managing and mitigating the variability of costs requires an understanding of how location, timing, and regional practices affect the price of electricity.

If you want to look up the average energy rates charged by utilities in your zip code, I recommend visiting the data catalog section of Data.gov, where you can download comprehensive spreadsheets with loads of valuable information.[3] Even if you aren't interested in the nitty-gritty details, it's critical to know that electricity costs are variable and inconsistent across the nation. Sometimes the reasons for these variations are self-evident and sometimes they make little sense whatsoever.

Electricity prices in the Northeast, for example, are significantly higher than prices in the rest of the country. Despite the region's proximity to areas rich in energy-producing resources, such as natural gas, coal, nuclear, hydropower, solar, and wind, the cost of electricity in the Northeast remains comparatively high.

Here's a snapshot of average electricity prices, in cents per kWh, for customers in all sectors of the energy economy (residential, commercial, industrial, and transportation) by region, excerpted from the EIA's February 2020 *Electric Power Monthly* report:[4]

Region	Cents per kWh
New England	18.22
Middle Atlantic	11.96
East North Central	9.90
West North Central	9:13
South Atlantic	9.86
East South Central	9.23
West South Central	8.11
Mountain	8.86
Pacific Contiguous	13.42
Pacific Noncontiguous	25.50

Source: US Energy Information Administration.

With the exception of the Pacific Noncontiguous region, which includes Hawaii and Alaska, the Northeast clearly leads the rest of the nation in electricity prices.

The explanation for that region's high cost of electricity is complex. Because New England is the oldest area of the country, infrastructure is often outdated and inadequate. The natural gas pipelines put in place are not large enough to handle the capacity of natural gas needed to produce the electricity and serve regular natural gas customers for production and heating uses, and thus New England experiences elevated prices.

An upgrade in the natural gas pipelines is underway, but adding capacity is a long and expensive process. Additionally, natural vegetation combined with volatile weather patterns lead to recurring damage and destruction of existing power infrastructure, which makes it difficult to stabilize electricity production effectively.

A Patchwork of Grids

Utility transmission companies are primarily private enterprises, which gives them vast leeway in setting their rate and pricing structures. Moreover, each state regulates energy differently, which makes it extremely difficult to craft national energy policies.

Unlike some nations, we don't have a national grid. Some grids serve an entire state, and others serve multiple states. Each grid has its own approach to sourcing energy, which adds complexity and variability to pricing.

Bewildering combinations of private entities, government organizations, and consumer groups lead to serial misunderstandings, lost opportunities, and a general sense of confusion. It shouldn't take an advanced degree to figure out your power bill, but that's the reality of our situation.

What about Fracking?

Fracking refers to the process by which gas is extracted from the earth by injecting a high-pressure water mixture that fractures the rock enabling gas release. Fracking has led to a boom in shale natural gas production, which has resulted in dramatic reductions in natural gas prices.

Fracking is controversial, however; it poses long-term environmental risks, and it has generated extensive political debate. Power plants are usually powered by natural gas, coal, or, occasionally, oil. Natural gas is now less expensive or equal in cost to oil or coal, and it produces less carbon output; consequently, many power plants want to convert to run on natural gas.

In the Northeast, however, a lack of existing infrastructure to transport the necessary natural gas from gas-producing states leads to generally higher prices and price spikes. Demand surges on cold winter days, when gas is used to heat homes and commercial buildings in addition to running manufacturing and industrial process equipment and to power generation plants, and on warm summer days, when natural gas is used to produce electricity and electricity is used primarily for cooling. Whenever the temperature drops or rises to uncomfortable levels, the price of natural gas skyrockets, which then affects the price of electricity.

Power Plant Decommissioning

Power plants don't last forever. Eventually, they are decommissioned and shut down, usually because they have become obsolete or grossly inefficient. Plants are also decommissioned to address concerns over immediate public health and safety risks and long-term environmental damage.

Decommissioning isn't a rare phenomenon. Here's a list of nuclear power plants that were in the process of being decommissioned in May 2020:

Name	Location
Crystal River—Unit 3	Crystal River, FL
Dresden—Unit 1	Morris, IL
Fermi—Unit 1	Newport, MI
Fort Calhoun	Fort Calhoun, NE
General Electric Co.—ESADA Vallecitos Experimental Superheat Reactor (EVESR)	Sunol, CA
General Electric Co.—Vallecitos Boiling Water Reactor (VBWR)	Sunol, CA
Humboldt Bay	Eureka, CA
Indian Point—Unit 1	Buchanan, NY
Kewaunee	Kewaunee, WI
LaCrosse Boiling Water Reactor	Genoa, WI
Millstone—Unit 1	Waterford, CT
Nuclear Ship Savannah	Baltimore, MD
Oyster Creek	Forked River, NJ
Peach Bottom—Unit 1	Delta, PA
San Onofre—Unit 1	San Clemente, CA
San Onofre—Units 2 and 3	San Clemente, CA
Three Mile Island—Unit 2	Middletown, PA
Vermont Yankee	Vernon, VT
Zion—Units 1 and 2	Zion, IL

Source: Nuclear Regulatory Commission.[5]

In many instances, decommissioning a plant pushes up electricity costs for customers who had been dependent on power from the plant. Again, there is no free lunch. Decommissioning a power plant doesn't reduce or eliminate the need for the electricity it had provided. The demand for power doesn't evaporate when a plant is decommissioned.

That said, there are clear trends in decommissioning. Coal and nuclear power plants are losing ground to plants fueled by natural gas and renewables. The current downward trend in coal-fired generation began in 2007, when increased US production of natural gas (particularly from shale) led to a sustained downward shift in natural gas spot prices. This resulted in an increase of production from natural gas-fired generators. In April 2015, traditionally the month when total electricity demand is lowest, US generation of electricity fueled by natural gas exceeded coal-fired generation for the first time since the start of EIA's monthly data generation in 1973.

Where Do Renewables Fit In?

Renewable energy sources produce less carbon than nonrenewable sources and reduce reliance on fossil fuels. Solar, wind, and hydropower are renewable sources of energy. Fuel cells, cogeneration plants, and bio fuel (which are cleaner than oil and coal) are also sometimes categorized as renewable energy sources. The degree of carbon produced directly correlates to how the state categorizes the energy source. In Connecticut, for example, there are three classes of renewables:

Class I: Solar, wind, fuel cells, geothermal, biogas, ocean, certain biomass, certain hydro, low-emission renewable energy conversion devices

Class II: Trash-to-energy, certain biomass, older run-of-river hydro

Class III: Certain combined heat and power (CHP), energy efficiency, waste heat

Each megawatt (MW) of electricity produced from a renewable energy source equates to the production of a Renewable Energy Certificate (REC). States with Renewable Portfolio Standards (RPS) mandate the percentage of electricity consumed that must be from renewable resources. If the supplier does not produce the renewable energy, then retiring a REC is how the RPS is fulfilled.

In most Northeastern states, renewable energy must account for roughly a quarter of total electricity generation. For example, in Connecticut, the mandate is 27 percent by 2020; in Massachusetts, it is 22.1 percent by 2020.[6]

To achieve these goals, Massachusetts installed 1312 MW of energy capacity from wind, solar, hydropower, and biomass in 2013.[7] Rhode Island is also in the process of installing a large percentage of their power from various renewable sources, and it will soon be part of a 1GW wind project.[8] Because the Northeast has high electricity costs in general, some energy sources such as biomass power plants, large-scale fuel cells, and wind power have reached what is known as price parity.[9] Price parity occurs when the cost of producing electricity from a certain source is equal to the general cost of producing electricity. In other words, it is not more expensive to buy electricity that is made from wind.

Although dependable pricing and local generation are great in the medium and long term, renewable energy does cost money in the short term for a variety of reasons. In more proactive states, renewable energy mandates will cost money because the state subsidizes and helps finance renewable energy system construction, with finance charges adding to the cost. Cape Wind, in Massachusetts, the nation's first off-shore wind farm, will power more than 75 percent of Cape Cod, Martha's Vineyard, and Nantucket. When it is particularly windy, electricity will be available to the surrounding states. However, this project will cost $2.6 billion, and even though most funding will come from private sources, the government still has to pitch in.[10] Other states, such as Connecticut, are not close to reaching their targets. This means they have to effectively "import" renewable energy at a cost from neighboring states or subsidize projects within Connecticut with ZREC or LREC (zero or low emissions REC) payments to make the project more attractive to the owner.

Multiple Factors Drive Energy Markets

What does the future hold? Anyone who tells you they know is either lying or woefully ignorant. Here's what we know: energy markets are dependent on a variety of determining factors:

- **What new projects will come online?** Deepwater Wind, Cape Wind, and biomass replacements for Vermont Yankee and Salem Harbor, among other projects, will affect electricity prices.

- **What infrastructure will be built?** Natural gas pipelines are rapidly being constructed to reach the Northeast. Electricity transmission lines are also being built from Québec to New Hampshire for the transmission of hydropower. Both projects will stabilize or lower energy costs when completed. Additionally, infrastructure is regularly being built throughout the country to improve both the flow of energy supply and the transmission lines to move the supply. Energy generation projects are also increasingly creating energy supply in the vicinity of generation facilities.

- **Continuing energy market deregulation.** Allowing deregulation was a federal decision, but deregulation laws are individual to each state, and hence they change regularly throughout the country. It is important to keep track of the changes, as they directly affect your meter.

- **Continuing energy-efficiency improvements.** Technology, lighting, mechanical, and building-enveloping equipment will continue to become more energy efficient. For example, a lighting retrofit today that saved 25 percent in kWh can likely be repeated in five years to save an additional 25 percent in kWh, and so on.

- **Market shocks:** War and political turbulence, especially in oil- and natural gas–producing countries, wreak havoc on energy markets.

Endnotes

1. https://www.eia.gov/todayinenergy/detail.php?id=42655
2. https://www.eia.gov/tools/faqs/faq.php?id=427&t=6
3. https://catalog.data.gov/dataset/u-s-electric-utility-companies-and -rates-look-up-by-zipcode-2018
4. https://www.eia.gov/electricity/monthly/epm_table_grapher .php?t=epmt_5_6_a
5. https://www.nrc.gov/info-finder/decommissioning/power -reactor/
6. http://instituteforenergyresearch.org/wp-content/uploads /2011/01/IER-RPS-Study-Final.pdf
7. http://www.acore.org/files/pdfs/states/Massachusetts.pdf
8. http://www.acore.org/files/pdfs/states/RhodeIsland.pdf
9. http://energy.gov/sites/prod/files/2015/11/f27/Revolution-Now -11132015.pdf
10. http://www.businessweek.com/articles/2014-07-11/government -money-is-not-silver-bullet-for-cape-wind-offshore-project

Chapter 10

Understand Your Energy Bills

I cannot overstate the importance of understanding your power bills. Commercial and industrial energy bill statements will have two distinct components: the electric generation/supply charge (depending on how the utility company describes the charge) and the transmission/distribution charge. The generation/supply portion is the actual energy charge, which is determined and charged in kWh (kilowatt-hours) for electricity, and in therms (0.10 MMbtu) or ccf (100 cubic feet of natural gas) for natural gas; it specifies the amount of energy consumption, the cost, and the source of energy.

The transmission/distribution charges are for the infrastructure needed to move the energy from the point of energy creation to the end-use location, including local wires, transformers, substations, and other necessities to deliver the energy. This is also called the distribution channels. These distribution channels for transmission/distribution are usually owned and operated by the utility company. A utility company may be either privately or municipally owned, or in some towns a combination of partial municipal and partial private ownership is in place.

Calculating the Cost of Demand

Demand rate is measured in kW (kilowatts) and calculated by the utility company. The demand rate or charge, which for industrial or commercial customers is listed separately in the transmission and distribution section, can be as much as 30 percent of your bill. In addition to being a significant cost to the company, demand is a heavy burden on the grid.

The distinction between demand (reported in kW) and consumption or energy use (reported in kWh) is an important concept. For commercial or industrial customers, the utility company bills separately for time-of-use (TOU) meters, which show company consumption patterns and peak demand. TOU meters record both kW and kWh. Electric demand, from an industrial or commercial perspective, refers to the maximum amount of *electrical energy* that is being consumed at a given time. The *demand in kW* will measure the highest average *demand* in any fifteen-minute period during the month. The fifteen-minute interval recorded with the highest demand overall will dictate the demand cost directly. All business owners and ratepayers should make a goal to reduce their peak demand and stabilize the demand load.

As an example of the difference between demand and consumption, consider the following example: a 100 W bulb turned on for ten hours will consume 1 kWh of electricity, with a demand on the grid of 100 W. Ten 100 W bulbs operating for one hour will consume 1 kWh of electricity, the same consumption as the first part of the example, but now the demand is 1000 W, and the utility company must have ten times the generating capacity to meet that demand. High demand requires more services from the utility in the form of additional generating capacity and more infrastructure, such as lines, transformers, and substation equipment.

A one-year history of kW and kWh use is typically specified on the utility bill, broken down by month. Make sure to check if the history for electricity is in kW or kWh (a reflection of energy demand or consumption). It is important to review the history and if use seems inconsistent, part of the building may not be functioning correctly. Many small business energy-efficiency funds will ask for monthly demand or kW information, which can be found on the bill.

There are several ways to either reduce or stabilize a company's energy demand, and these types of adjustments will have a significant impact on energy costs. Energy management systems can be set so that when a certain demand is reached, the system compensates and draws energy from alternate sources to stabilize the demand on the grid. This would ensure the company does not incur any spikes in demand, and in turn this will save money by stabilizing the demand load over time. Energy management systems can also stabilize demand load by incorporating a backup battery system that stores energy. When a threshold demand level is reached, the system would switch to the battery and come off the grid, avoiding spikes in demand and keeping the demand profile stable. This will ultimately reduce overall cost. Awareness of energy demand, demand cost, and the impact of stabilizing demand will help business owners make better choices about whether to replace or repair high demand-consuming process equipment or mechanicals, and this, in turn, will lower the largest portion of the energy bill.

Contributions to energy-efficiency funds are also detailed in the total delivery charges section of your bill. This money is collected from each ratepayer and it is a source of funding available to all ratepayers to subsidize energy-efficiency projects. Often up to 40 percent of the cost can be given back to the ratepayer. Figures 10.1 and 10.2 (at the end of this chapter) are examples of an energy bill showing the itemized charges in detail.

Impact of Energy Deregulation

The deregulation of energy has divided the utility company monopolies by separating the production of energy from the distribution. This separation creates more competition. Prior to this deregulation, both electricity and natural gas were provided by local utilities or regional monopolies that controlled the power generation and distribution channels for delivery (www.deregulationofenergy.org). As a result of energy deregulation, clients can, but do not have to, choose their electricity or natural gas supply company from an alternative supply company to the distribution channel. The following states are deregulated for electricity:

- California (partially deregulated)
- Connecticut
- Delaware
- Illinois
- Maine

- Maryland
- Massachusetts
- Michigan
- Montana
- New Hampshire
- New Jersey
- New York
- Ohio
- Oregon
- Pennsylvania
- Rhode Island
- Texas
- District of Columbia

If you are located in one of the deregulated electric or gas states, you may choose to purchase your energy supply from an alternative supplier company that is not your utility company or distribution channel. The general consensus is that deregulation may currently be effectively lowering prices for the first time since its introduction. It is important to understand the factors when considering an alternative supply company because alternative supply companies are *not always cheaper* than the utility company.

Considerations before Choosing Alternative Suppliers

Alternative suppliers can provide benefits not offered by traditional suppliers, but you need to do your homework. Here are some of the challenges and opportunities you should know before choosing a supplier:

- **Working with a broker or directly with a supply company.** If you choose a supply company to work with directly, they are offering you what they have available. If you choose to work with a broker, they are a middle person and as such will be adding a cost to your supply charge to pay for their service. The broker can offer you more than one supply company's product. If you sign a letter of exclusivity with a broker firm, you are limiting your ability to price your own electric supply with other supply companies, and more significantly, you are now locked into whatever additional cost or margin the broker chooses to add onto the supply company's cost. Additionally, some brokers will add language to their contracts stating that even if the contract is discontinued, the broker fee will still be charged. It is advisable to find a broker who does not require an exclusivity clause or who charges additional fees—deregulation is intended to afford you choice and competitive pricing.

- **The broker fee.** Electric supply companies compensate brokers by paying the broker in mils (a unit of currency equal to 1/10th of a penny), which is added to the customer's supply cost. An example of the math: every 0.001 mil added to the price of 1,000,000 kWh (1MW) will equal $1,000.00 for the broker. Wise businesspeople will ask brokers to disclose the mils and corresponding dollar amounts they are receiving from supply companies. The broker fee amount is negotiable and the recommendation is to offer the broker a reasonable flat fee for the service. The time required to price the supply is easily quantifiable, and once the contract is signed, there will be no additional work for the broker.

- **Supply cost components.** All component costs can be included in the supply cost. This is called an all-in price. Individual components (the equivalent to baggage fees and fuel assessments in airline ticket costs, for example) can be priced separately as well, fixing some of the costs and floating some with the market to avoid paying the higher, premium all-inclusive cost. Either way, awareness of what is included in the price and clarification of the arrangement in writing is key.

- **Tolerance in the supply quantity variation.** Each supply company has a different tolerance for how much your electric supply requirements can change within the contract period. Typically, electric supply pricing takes into account a company's supply history over the previous twelve months, and this estimate is then projected into the future year. If the use requirement (or bandwidth, as it is sometimes called) changes, you may be charged a penalty. Electric supply contracts might have a bandwidth clause or, conversely, full requirement contracts will supply all electricity needs at the contracted rate.

- **Electric meter or account changes.** From time to time, a company will receive a new meter or a new account number. This information must be communicated to your supply company in order for the contracted rate to be applied to the new account or meter number. The utility company has no way of connecting the two, so the supply company must inform the utility.

- **Termination fees.** Most electric energy supply contracts have termination fees. It is important to understand the contract meter start and stop dates and whether there will be a termination fee if you leave the supply company before the end date. Often, start-stop dates can be confusing. For instance, you may sign a contract on a certain date, assuming the contract begins that month, but because you missed the meter read for that month, the price change won't take effect until the following month. Utility companies usually change the supply rate on the monthly meter read date, which is different for each meter and hence it is essential to learn how to verify your meter read date. Expect that from the date you sign the contract, you will need to wait a minimum of seven to ten business days before your price change for that meter-read cycle is applied and sent in to the utility company through the EDI (electronic data interchange).

- **Electric supply costs.** Electric supply costs are not continually going up. Energy supply costs at the time of the writing of this book are lower than they were in 2009 and most years thereafter. Despite what salespeople may say, electric supply cost will not necessarily go up each year; historical utility data support this, and business executives can further confirm this by reviewing utility supply charges for their particular business over time.

- **Understanding the utility company's electric supply rate for each meter.** Some utility companies price the supply monthly, others quarterly, some semiannually, and others annually. It is important to understand the utility company pricing and when price changes will happen.

Looking back at three years of historical utility company pricing for a particular rate class will likely show trends in pricing that correlate with times of the year.

■ **Consider cost savings and budget stability when exploring utility pricing.** Once utility pricing and historical rates are taken into consideration, the likelihood of saving money from an alternative supply company or receiving price stability for budgeting purposes can be determined. Data show most people are not saving money with alternative supply companies despite claims from sales personnel. Due diligence in this area can result in real cost savings.

■ **Energy supply contracts.** It is best to appoint a specific person within a company with the authority to execute energy supply contracts. Given the potential cost of uninformed decisions and the need to have energy contracts reviewed by legal counsel, executive management teams will benefit from having designated individuals manage these types of contractual documents.

Pricing Is Problematic but Cannot Be Ignored

Generally speaking, even the most up-to-date, efficient buildings have to use some electricity or natural gas. Pricing correctly has the potential to reduce energy costs by a substantial percentage without even having to lower energy use. Following are some basic pricing tactics:

■ Know your utility company's supply rate and how often the supply rate would change.

- Understand, when pricing an alternative contract, what the contract length is and question if changing the contract length can save you money, because you are now incorporating a shoulder season.
- Acknowledge the differences in pricing times and costs between the utility and alternative suppliers in your state, if applicable.
- Understand risk.
- Understand termination fees.

In Connecticut, the utility company generally releases electric rates two times per year, in December and June. The December rates apply from January to June, and the June rates apply from July to December. Most other states follow a similar schedule as well, though some monthly and some quarterly. When the utility rates come out, price check them against alternative suppliers. *The utility rate is not always more expensive.*

Volatility and contract length make a huge difference. Many factors lead to price increases, and energy costs can seesaw over the time of year. Because the utility rates are set on a schedule, it can be difficult to predict costs past what the known costs are. Alternative energy suppliers can price one-, two-, and three-year contracts or some other variation of time.

Pricing in different seasons can help tremendously. Spring and fall are known as the shoulder seasons, and electricity is often, but not always, less expensive to price in these seasons than in the winter and summer. Abnormally cool stretches in the summer and abnormally warm periods in the winter result in lower energy prices. This is not guaranteed, but it can happen.

Politics and global events quickly change energy prices. Events such as conflicts in the Middle East, Russia, and Venezuela, for example, can make prices more volatile (and higher) in the short term.

Shop around for suppliers: Energy is slowly becoming a more perfect market. Looking around at a variety of suppliers can ensure that you've found the most competitive rates. By not signing an exclusivity agreement you are giving yourself the option to price and affording yourself the best visibility into pricing.

Rate Class and Charges

Commercial customers are assigned rate classes based on their energy use. A company's rate class may have a large effect on its energy bill, and companies should review their rate class on an annual basis. In Connecticut, Eversource and UI vary their rates based on rate class. As an example, for the second half of 2014, UI charged a 0.221¢/kWh difference in the peak and off-peak rates of LPT (large power fifteen-minute time interval meter time of use) and GST (general service fifteen-minute time interval meter time of use), with the GST service being less expensive.[1]

Commercial customers who are undergoing energy-efficiency measures or have widely varying energy use are especially encouraged to review their rate class because it is most likely to have changed. The utility meter rate class is specified on the bill, and it determines the cost class structure for supply and transmission of energy. Becoming familiar with the correct rate class and reviewing this information annually will help to avoid inappropriate charges. By reviewing annually, changes in production that occur from time to time, and subsequent rate class changes based on the new production, can be monitored. Consult with companies that specialize in utility bill review (which work on a commission basis).

The TOU meter can also be a helpful device to monitor energy-consumption patterns; this type of meter will show what portion of the energy consumed was used on- and off-peak in fifteen-minute measurements. This information is useful to budget energy consumption more efficiently.

What about Natural Gas?

Natural gas, a versatile and relatively inexpensive fossil fuel, is replacing petroleum in many key energy venues. Natural gas is used mostly in commercial HVAC systems and for power generation. Cogeneration and fuel cell systems often use natural gas as well.

It's important to understand the differences between natural gas pricing and electricity pricing. Unlike electricity, which is generated, natural gas is a resource, and the market for natural gas responds directly to supply and demand. As previously mentioned, the Northeast does not have sufficient infrastructure to get the proper amount of natural gas into the area. As a result, when gas is in extremely high demand, such as on the coldest days of winter, the market price rises sharply. However, pricing is generally made on a monthly basis, so customers are sometimes not affected by such rapid price increases.

When customers choose an alternative natural gas company, they must stay there for one year before they can return to their utility company for natural gas supply. And if customers return to a utility company for supply, they cannot return to the alternative company for supply for one year. As stated, natural gas prices vary monthly, with no forward visibility in pricing. Market trends are used for decision-making.

Energy Is Subject to Sales Tax

Utility bills reflect taxes and credits as well, and it is essential to continually monitor tax charges for accuracy. The bill should reflect tax-exempt status, and a tax-exempt status for energy purchases is not the same as being a not-for-profit 501c3 entity.

Tax-exempt status can be based on being a manufacturer or industrial business, a small business, a nursing home, and for many other reasons determined by the state. Each state's revenue service division defines which entities are tax-exempt for energy purchases, and this can often be a pleasant surprise to business owners. The tax exemption often applies to all energy sources, such as electricity, natural gas, propane, oil, and so on. In addition, if you are being taxed improperly, in many states you can recuperate the last thirty-six months of incorrect tax charges and receive a credit on your bill in addition to relieving yourself of the tax charge going forward.

In Connecticut, the Department of Revenue Services CERT-115 provides exemptions for certain purchases of gas, electricity, and heating fuel for residential, agricultural, manufacturing, and industrial customers. New York State exempts energy purchases on the condition that the energy goes directly to the manufacturing and the industrial process. (The exact rules are defined in Publication 852, page 17, of the New York State Department of Taxation and Finance.) Massachusetts has a similar exemption for all manufacturers and small businesses.

Endnote

1. http://www.uinet.com/wps/portal/uinet/customercare/

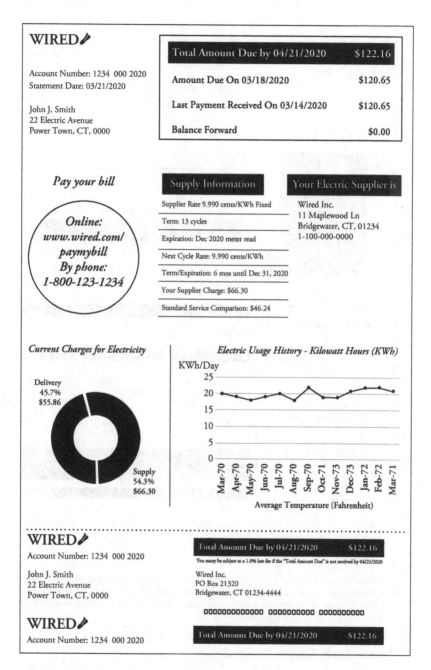

Figure 10.1 Sample Energy Bill A

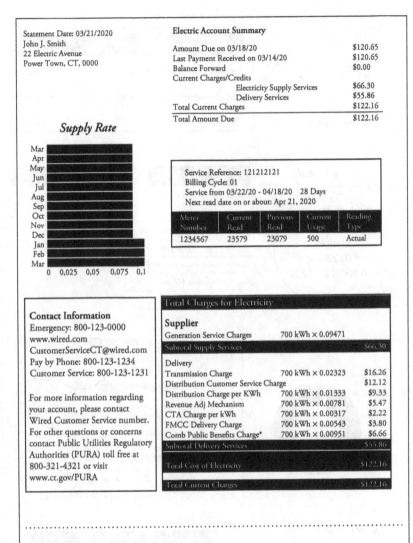

Statement Date: 03/21/2020
John J. Smith
22 Electric Avenue
Power Town, CT, 0000

Electric Account Summary

Amount Due on 03/18/20	$120.65
Last Payment Received on 03/14/20	$120.65
Balance Forward	$0.00
Current Charges/Credits	
Electricity Supply Services	$66.30
Delivery Services	$55.86
Total Current Charges	$122.16
Total Amount Due	$122.16

Supply Rate

Mar
Apr
May
Jun
Jul
Aug
Sep
Oct
Nov
Dec
Jan
Feb
Mar

0   0,025   0,05   0,075   0,1

Service Reference: 121212121
Billing Cycle: 01
Service from 03/22/20 - 04/18/20   28 Days
Next read date on or about: Apr 21, 2020

Meter Number	Current Read	Previous Read	Current Usage	Reading Type
1234567	23579	23079	500	Actual

Contact Information
Emergency: 800-123-0000
www.wired.com
CustomerServiceCT@wired.com
Pay by Phone: 800-123-1234
Customer Service: 800-123-1231

For more information regarding
your account, please contact
Wired Customer Service number.
For other questions or concerns
contact Public Utilities Regulatory
Authorities (PURA) toll free at
800-321-4321 or visit
www.ct.gov/PURA

Total Charges for Electricity

Supplier

Generation Service Charges	700 kWh × 0.09471	
Subtotal Supply Services		$66.30

Delivery

Transmission Charge	700 kWh × 0.02323	$16.26
Distribution Customer Service Charge		$12.12
Distribution Charge per KWh	700 kWh × 0.01333	$9.33
Revenue Adj Mechanism	700 kWh × 0.00781	$5.47
CTA Charge per kWh	700 kWh × 0.00317	$2.22
FMCC Delivery Charge	700 kWh × 0.00543	$3.80
Comb Public Benefits Charge*	700 kWh × 0.00951	$6.66
Subtotal Delivery Services		$55.86
Total Cost of Electricity		$122.16
Total Current Charges		$122.16

Explanation of your charges

*The Combined Public Benefits Charge represents a combination of three charges formerly known as: Conservation and Load Mgmt Charge, Renewable Energy Investment Charge, and System Benefits Charge. This charge also includes the Conservation Adjustment Mechanism approved by the Public Utilities Regulatory Authorities

Figure 10.2 Sample Energy Bill B

Chapter 11

Find the Money

We're all motivated by self-interest. It's part of our basic survival mechanism, and there's no point in denying the role that self-interest plays in all of our decision-making processes.

Energy conservation and energy-efficiency programs are unlikely to succeed unless they demonstrate clear short-term benefits. Fortunately, the energy economy is richly stocked with a multitude of financial incentives that make conservation and efficiency highly logical choices for companies and individuals. Essentially, these incentives are rewards for good behavior and it makes sense to employ them.

Money is everywhere—but you have to know where to look. Numerous economic incentives are available for conserving energy, using energy more efficiently, and generating energy without harming the environment. This chapter will give you a brief overview of the many financial opportunities that already exist and can be tapped into.

It's important to note that these incentives can be layered, resulting in additive cost reductions. For example, a project could potentially receive local cash incentives from an energy-efficiency fund, qualify for a federal tax deduction, while being financed 100 percent with a 0 percent interest rate loan—assuming that specific prerequisites and submission deadlines are carefully followed.

In the United States, taxes are regulated and administered at the federal, state, and municipal levels. Each level treats energy differently. The federal government and individual state governments provide tax exemptions, deductions, depreciation deductions, and tax credits. The federal tax benefit for energy conservation projects is derived from tax deductions under Section 179D of the Internal Revenue Code for Commercial Building Tax Deductions, and the federal tax benefit for energy generation is in the form of investment tax credits.

State tax advantages can be in several formats, most commonly as a sales tax exemption or a tax credit. (Refer to the DSIRE website [www.dsireusa.org] for your particular state's tax.)

Federal Tax Credits

The federal government provides significant energy corporate tax credit programs such as the Business Energy Investment Tax Credit (ITC). The ITC covers up to 30 percent of expenditures for solar, fuel cell, and small wind turbine systems. It also covers up to 10 percent of expenditures toward geothermal systems, microturbines, and combined heat and power (or CHP) systems. The ITC was initially set up to run through 2016, but it has been extended beyond this expiration date through 2021 to the benefit of the business energy consumer.[1]

A well-funded tax credit is the Qualifying Advanced Energy Manufacturing Investment Tax Credit. This investment tax credit covers 30 percent of any qualified investment (one specifically listed in the tax code) in energy efficiency or renewable energy-generation manufacturing.[2]

Federal Depreciation and Tax

Businesses can recover some of the investments made on their property through depreciation deductions. The Modified Accelerated Cost-Recovery System (MACRS) is the current tax depreciation system in the United States. It establishes a set of class lives, from three to fifty years, over which an annual deduction can be claimed for property depreciation. These class lives are determined by the tax code and based on the theoretical life of the asset. Technologies and projects that qualify for MACRS are listed at the end of this chapter. Energy-generation projects can qualify for an accelerated MACRS program; for example, solar energy systems qualify for a five-year depreciation, benefiting business by depreciating the asset more quickly. In turn, the company sees greater tax savings in those years.

In addition to depreciation programs, the federal government has provided a tax deduction for capital projects relevant to energy-efficiency upgrades. The Federal Code section 179D tax deduction, which expired in 2013 and has now been reinstated retroactively to January 1, 2015, provides a deduction of up to $1.80/square foot for work building owners or ratepayers to create more energy-efficient commercial buildings.

There are three categories of energy-efficiency upgrades:

- Interior lighting systems
- Heating, cooling, ventilation, and hot water systems
- Building-envelope improvements

These upgrades must be certified to satisfy the energy-efficiency requirements of 179D(c)(1) and (d) of the Internal Revenue Code. Partial tax deductions are allowed for upgrades where at least one category is represented. For example: a building owner can earn a $0.60 per square foot deduction to upgrade the building's lighting systems. Each qualifying upgrade is worth one-third of the total allowable deduction. The upgrades must be placed in service the year you claim the tax deduction.

State Sales Tax Exemptions

In Connecticut, for example, the Department of Revenue Services CERT-115 provides exemptions for certain purchases of gas, electricity, and heating fuel for residential, agricultural, and industrial customers. This exemption applies specifically to any residential dwelling, as well as premises where 75 percent or more of energy use is for agricultural production, for the fabrication of a finished product or for industrial manufacturing. Please see reference details at the end of this chapter.

New York State exempts energy purchases on the condition that the energy goes directly to manufacturing and the industrial process. The exact rules are defined in Publication 852, page 17, of the New York State Department of Taxation and Finance. Massachusetts has a similar exemption for all manufacturers and small businesses.

Depending on your location, commercial, industrial, and residential customers should be aware of a variety of available sales tax exemptions on the purchase of gas, electricity, or heating fuel. Importantly, if an exemption is available and sales tax has been unduly charged, your company may have an opportunity to be reimbursed for up to 36 months of prior tax payments.

Sales and Use Tax Exemption for Solar and Geothermal Energy

Connecticut, Vermont, New York, Massachusetts, Rhode Island, and several other states offer a sales and use tax exemption for solar energy equipment and geothermal technologies. New Jersey has a similar sales tax exemption for solar technology only. Many other states, within and outside of the Northeast and Mid-Atlantic, have similar tax incentives.

Local Property Tax Exemptions

Connecticut, New York, Massachusetts, Rhode Island, Vermont, and New Jersey offer a property tax exemption for Class 1 renewable energy systems used to generate energy for commercial and industrial properties. The exemption is available on commercial properties for solar, wind, fuel cell, cogeneration, and geothermal systems, among others. In Pennsylvania, the exemption applies only to wind-derived energy systems. The status of this exemption per state can be verified with the Department of Revenue Services of the state.

Rebate Programs

Utility companies, and public benefit funds (PBFs) in Connecticut, such as CEEF (Connecticut Energy Efficiency Fund) and CMEEC (Connecticut Municipal Electric Energy Consortium), frequently offer rebates on certain energy-efficiency upgrades for items such as restaurant equipment, refrigeration, lighting, appliances, and cogeneration per KW purchased. Rebates are a stated amount of cash that will be paid to you once a project is completed. The rebate will typically require a form to be completed and often a receipt for payment and a contractor's signature verifying work completion will be required as well.

Here are some easy tips for making a rebate process go more smoothly:

- Check online or call your utility company program coordinator to find out the terms and conditions of the rebate. Many programs will apply to specific models and/or makes.
- Fill out the appropriate rebate application to ensure eligibility.

- Work with a verified contractor to install the appropriate unit(s).

- Submit the rebate application. This generally requires the contractor's signature confirming completion of the installation and a receipt for the paid model or unit.

- Check how long you have after the installation to submit necessary rebate documents and mark this date on your calendar. It is imperative to be aware of deadlines for application and submission of rebates because these can easily be forfeited.

If you do intend to access rebate dollars, it is important to read the rebate form carefully prior to beginning the project. Make sure you are using an appropriate licensed contractor if this is a prerequisite for the rebate and make sure you have access to itemized receipts for purchased materials, if required, especially if the materials are purchased by a contractor.

Contractors may mark up the cost of materials, making them reluctant to provide original receipts. The rebate requirements for itemized receipts should be discussed openly with the contractor up front to avoid issues or delays with the rebate submission.

Most rebates do not require prior notice or a letter of agreement (LOA) to a fund or rebate company administrator. It is still advisable that an administrator review the project to avoid purchasing a product that then does not qualify for the rebate. Rebates do change frequently, however, and fund administrators may point to additional rebates as well.

Cash Incentives

Cash incentives are available to encourage the adoption of strategies to reduce energy consumption. Incentive programs often require the involvement of a program account manager in the planning and design stage of the project, typically including a walk-through of the premises before any work is begun. Once the energy conservation project is chosen and discussed, the program account manager will provide the company a contract for the incentive award. This LOA states that if the company performs the energy-efficiency upgrades as noted within a specific period of time, a check will be awarded to the company within thirty days of the final walk-through. Often the cash incentive can be assigned to a contractor if the assignment is done in writing and specified on the form provided by the program. The LOA will address the following:

- Current energy consumption
- Projected energy consumption after project completion
- Energy savings
- Project cost
- Return on investment (ROI)
- Cash value of incentive on project completion and incentive delivery date
- Time line for project completion

Not all incentive money will require a LOA, but most will. Awareness of this potential requirement will avoid losing the opportunity to collect on cash incentive offers.

PBFs offer cash incentives financed from the public benefit surcharge on utility bills. For example, CEEF provides financial incentives as a way to reduce overall energy use through a combined public benefit charge that all Connecticut non-municipal ratepayers pay on their electricity and gas bills.

CEEF is not the only organization of its kind; institutions such as this exist outside of Connecticut as well. Massachusetts has the Massachusetts Clean Energy Center and the Renewable Energy Trust Fund, subsidized by a surcharge on electric utility bills, and other states have comparable counterparts.

The local utility company generally services the programs that provide incentives for energy efficiency and energy generation. A list of incentives is posted on utility company websites, with details on the energy conservation measures that qualify for the programs.

Always Follow the Guidelines

It is absolutely essential to follow all of the required steps. Nothing is more disappointing to me than hearing a client say, "We just completed a project," and then discovering they missed a step and can no longer obtain the incentive they had been expecting.

I strongly recommend designating an internal dedicated communicator as a point of contact with the utility company or the incentive fund representative. The designated person should meet with the fund administrator regularly to discuss intended capital projects.

Additional money is often available for process or equipment projects, such as upgrading computer hard drives, switching a DC motor to AC, obtaining a new copier, or putting outside timers on parking lot lights. Establishing a working relationship with the fund administrator is time well spent, frequently translating into a simpler process overall and potentially additional incentive cash.

When using cash incentives, always remember that each program has very specific requirements. Be sure to confirm that you are purchasing the model or properly designated item that qualifies for the incentive. For example, the incentive fund may require that LED lighting is specifically Energy Star approved. You would not want to have a purchasing agent or contractor purchase non–Energy Star LEDs for the same cost and then learn that the items are not eligible—a potentially lost opportunity to earn cash for the company. A meeting to consult with the fund administrator prior to finalizing project decisions could avoid these types of mishaps.

Here's another important fact that's often overlooked: When multiple energy conservation projects are bundled together, a company can receive an extra cash bonus.

Spend Time on the DSIRE Website

You're probably getting tired of me mentioning the DSIRE website, but it's a genuinely critical part of your process for identifying and obtaining incentives. DSIRE provides comprehensive lists of incentives at every level. By going to the DSIRE website and clicking "view federal incentives," you can see a general list of nationwide incentives. The website also collects state and utility incentives by location—scroll over and click on each state to see incentives in your area.

Demand Response Program

Electric demand, from an industrial or commercial perspective, refers to the maximum amount of electrical energy that is being consumed at a given time. Demand is stated in kW. With a time of use meter, demand is measured by the electric meter as the highest average demand in any fifteen-minute period during the month. The utility company monitors demand closely from both the perspective of the individual meter and their portfolio as a whole. It is beneficial for all parties involved to reduce the overall demand on the grid. As the grid is able to lower demand, there is a reduction in the output required by the grid, lowering the cost to produce electricity and reducing the chance of outages. During times of heavy use, high demand is a burden to the system, which will in turn significantly increase cost to all stakeholders.

The need to reduce demand was the genesis of the demand response program. This program was instituted to lessen the demand on the grid during peak hours, and it can have a significant impact on your overall energy costs.

Utility companies are required to have the capacity to provide the energy you need. In order to estimate this need, the utility company reviews your bill and looks at the highest amount of demand for a given period of time. The utility company then projects that requirement to make sure they have that amount of energy available for you, should you need it. If your use is inconsistent with spikes in demand, you are charged a fee for the utility company's ability to cover that need for you at all times.

The fee can be expensive. The larger the delta (Δ, or the difference between the highest amount of demand and the lowest amount of demand), the higher the cost. In simple terms, the more stable and consistent you can keep your demand the less expensive your demand fees will be, because the utility company has to have less energy in reserve to cover your needs. You will be charged for your highest demand at all times, whether you use the energy or not.

A demand response program pays consumers to reduce kW, and companies will be paid to shed some of their load during a peak demand time. It requires the capacity to shut off a significant amount of your load at a moment's notice. A company will be compensated if they are able to do this as part of the demand response program.

If enough companies shed their load during peak use, the grid will not be required to switch to an alternate source of generation, such as possibly an oil or coal plant. In Connecticut, this program is managed by the Office of Policy and Management (OPM). The value of this deferred infrastructure to the grid operator, ISO New England, is demonstrated by the payment to OPM, through third-party contractors on behalf of forty sites at the eleven participating agencies, of approximately $429,000 per quarter. OPM distributes this money to the participating agencies for the promotion or installation of energy-saving projects.

Loans, Interest Rate Buy-Downs, and Specialized Financing

The first section of this chapter offered a high-level overview of the many incentives, rebates, tax credits, tax deductions, and exemptions available. The next section of this chapter focuses on options for financing energy-efficiency projects. My experience in the field has taught me that if you take the time to develop a plan for a viable project, you can usually find a reasonable way to finance it.

Public Benefit Funds

Many states throughout the country have created PBFs for the increased use of energy-efficient technologies and renewable energy. The State of Connecticut's CEEF was instated through Public Act 11-80 Section 33 and 13-298 Section 16 of the Connecticut General Assembly. More than twenty states have similar funds for renewable energy or energy efficiency. A good resource for further information on this and many other relevant topics is the Database for State Incentives for Renewable Energy or DSIRE.

PBFs can be a source of financing in several ways. The first, for smaller companies that use less than 200 kW per month and with good utility bill credit history, will qualify applicants for financing up to $100,000 at 0 percent interest for energy-efficiency projects, with a payback of less than five years. The second source of funding from a PBF can provide financing with a low-interest rate for larger projects, and the PBF buys down the interest rate for the company. This funding is available in excess of $1,000,000 per company per project.

Power Purchase Agreements

When setting up an energy generation system, a company can choose to allow a third party to own the energy generation project and sell back the energy produced. A power purchase agreement (PPA) is a contract created between the owner of the system and the ratepayer. The terms of the contract generally include the size of the system and the price of the energy (generally electricity).

A PPA essentially guarantees that the electricity produced by a system, such as wind, solar, fuel cell, or CHP, will be purchased at a certain price while allowing the ratepayer to obtain energy from a cleaner, more reliable source. Owners and ratepayers must be cautious; it is important to understand the PPA clearly to make certain that it is cost-effective. PPAs appear in this chapter because they are very often structured so that after a certain number of years, the ratepayer can acquire ownership of the system. This often makes the most sense for the original owner of the PPA when using solar panel systems; it is not reasonable or cost-effective to remove solar panels after twenty years of use.

Caveat emptor: PPAs typically build in interest or cost escalators to the pricing—these are arbitrary, cumulative escalations applied to the price of energy over time. There is no economic basis for this strategy, and it is somewhat of a trick of the trade. They can and should be removed from the agreement.

PPAs are not consistent about maintenance charges. Be mindful to understand if your PPA includes all maintenance, which should be your preference, or if maintenance will be an additional charge. If maintenance will be an additional charge, fix this charge for the life of the PPA because you should be aware of all costs at the time you implement the project.

Energy Supply Company Financing

Energy supply companies can also provide financing. Smaller companies, as well as national players such as Engie, Constellation Energy, and others will provide financing to a variety of energy conservation projects for their energy supply clients if the ROI fits their portfolio. The client then pays for the projects via an increased energy supply expense, affording the company an operating expense (OPEX) instead of debt in the form of a capital expense (CAPEX), typically a more palatable financial arrangement.

Property assessed clean energy (PACE) programs may also help companies finance energy-efficiency upgrades or renewable energy installations for buildings. PACE is still in development legislatively, and it is offered only in limited municipalities. C-PACE means it is a PACE program that applies only to commercial buildings.[3] PACE programs are largely available in California, Colorado, Connecticut, Florida, Maine, Michigan, Minnesota, Missouri, New York, Ohio, Vermont, Wisconsin, and the District of Columbia, among other states.

Examples of upgrades range from adding more attic insulation to installing rooftop solar panels. PACE allows building owners to finance qualifying energy efficiency and clean energy improvements through a voluntary assessment on their property tax bill. Property owners pay for the improvements over time through this additional charge on their property tax bill, and the repayment obligation transfers automatically to the next owner if the property is sold. Capital provided under the C-PACE program is secured by a lien on the property, so low-interest capital can be raised from the private sector.

Performance-Based Financing through an Energy Service Company

Energy supply companies and energy service companies are easily confused, and often both use the acronym ESCO. An ESCO, in this instance, is an energy service company that will energy benchmark, and then audit, your building with the intent to carry out and then pay for energy conservation and efficiency improvements. The company pays the ESCO via a shared savings program or other agreed-on term. Often, these contracts last ten to twenty years in order to repay the ESCO for the work performed.

If a company chooses this program, it should hire a separate measurement and verification firm to oversee the accurate representation of all work. Additionally, the company should be sure to add a clause in the contract to account for any change in energy production or hours of operation.

These types of fluctuations will affect energy consumption independently of the work performed on the building, and the company has no need to share any energy savings that result from these types of operation/production changes. The upside is that the building outlays no cash or capital; the negative is risk and interest charges. If the building requires a small project with a ROI of less than four years, there is probably another financing option that would require no outlay of cash or capital.

Good Sources of Local Information

If you have an idea for a project for your company, a multitude of people can provide guidance. Calling the utility company's energy conservation and efficiency department and requesting an account manager is a good beginning. The state energy department or the state regulatory authority responsible for energy can provide information as well. Both the utility company and state government agencies should be aware of existing programs to help with project funding through an energy fund or PACE program; private banks and capital providers would have to be sourced separately and energy project funding is available through these sources.

Evaluating Energy Savings of Completed Projects

Energy savings are easiest seen from energy benchmarking prior to beginning projects and annually after completion. Energy calculations derived from benchmarking data will determine and confirm energy savings.

Almost all financial opportunities to fund energy savings projects require a calculation of energy consumed before and after the updates. This is no cause for alarm. The contractor or the fund administrator can make these calculations. A company's internal energy manager or an outsourced energy management firm can also deliver these energy metrics.

An initial step is understanding which calculations are required. Product data are needed to perform these calculations, and for this reason, meeting with the fund administrator at the project planning stage will ensure the appropriate product is chosen.

Before-and-after energy calculations are not necessary if purchasing a new item rather than replacing or updating an old one. If you are purchasing a new piece of inventory or a new system for your building, it is important to confirm these qualify as acceptable product models or systems from the specific fund lists. We again recommend contacting the administrator of the fund and reviewing the intended purchase or updated plans to confirm no minor changes are needed to capture the cash.

* * *

The economic opportunities described in this chapter apply to the following types of energy-efficiency projects:

- Equipment insulation
- Water heaters
- Lighting
- Lighting controls/sensors
- Energy management systems
- Building management systems
- Chillers
- Furnaces
- Boilers
- Heat pumps
- Central air conditioners
- Caulking/weather-stripping
- Duct/air sealing
- Building insulation
- Windows/window film, window inserts
- Roofs
- Industrial steam cleaners
- Tankless water heaters
- Heat pump water heaters
- DC to AC motor conversion in process equipment
- VFD and VAD
- Solar water heat
- Solar space heat
- Solar thermal electric
- Solar thermal process heat

- Solar photovoltaics
- Battery storage
- Landfill gas
- Wind
- Biomass
- Geothermal electric
- Fuel cells
- Geothermal heat pumps
- Municipal solid waste
- CHP/cogeneration
- Solar hybrid lighting

- Hydrokinetic power
- Anaerobic digestion
- Tidal energy
- Wave energy
- Ocean thermal
- Fuel cells using renewable fuels
- Microturbines
- Geothermal direct-use
- Ethanol
- Biodiesel

Choosing Your Project

When you consider the need for energy efficiency and the abundance of financial incentives, there's simply no excuse for inaction. If you own a home or building, my advice is to pick an energy project and get started today. Here's a quick list of questions to ask yourself:

- Where and how does your building fail to be energy efficient?
- What have you not updated in a significant amount of time?
- Are you using oil when you could be using natural gas?
- Are you in an area with competitive renewable energy options?
- Is your energy demand suitable for a fuel cell of a cogeneration system?

Once you have an idea for a project, find the available federal, state, and local incentives. The easiest way to accomplish this is by visiting the DSIRE website (www.dsireusa.org).

Here are some quick steps I recommend for using DSIRE:

■ Click on the state in which the project will be carried out, or click on "federal incentives."

■ Scroll through the utility company and state incentives.

■ Click on any pertinent incentives.

■ Ensure that the efficiency technology or renewable technology is eligible and that the company sector is applicable.

■ Check feasibility.

■ Look on the incentive page for the monetary amount of incentive listed. The price after incentives can then be used to check for return on investment and feasibility.

Endnotes

1. https://www.energystar.gov/about/federal_tax_credits/renewable_energy_tax_credits

2. https://www.blacklinegrp.com/blog/tax-incentives-for-manufacturing-businesses

3. https://greenworkslending.com/what-is-c-pace/

Chapter 12

Educate and Communicate

I believe wholeheartedly that using energy more carefully and more efficiently can put money in your pocket, make you a happier person, and create a cascade of benefits for the world we inhabit together. If you've read this far, you probably hold similar beliefs.

But what good are our beliefs unless we act on them? What's the point of acquiring knowledge if we don't share it? How can we make genuine progress if we only talk with people who already agree with us?

In this chapter, we'll take a look at techniques and advice for sharing the message, raising awareness, and dealing with naysayers. Some effort will be required, which is natural. Our culture has enjoyed nearly unlimited access to energy resources, and over time we have developed many wasteful habits. As previously mentioned, nearly 68 percent of the total energy consumed in the United States is wasted, according to Lawrence Livermore National Laboratory.[1]

Changing the long-standing habits of a culture won't be easy, but I'm confident we can shift the attitudes of enough people to make a lasting difference in how we generate power and consume energy. Fortunately, the tide of opinion is turning. Americans increasingly understand the connection between climate change and health issues.[2] A recent survey by the Pew Research Center shows that two-thirds of Americans see the negative impact of climate change on their communities and want the government to do more, "including large-scale tree planting efforts, tax credits for businesses that capture carbon emissions, and tougher fuel efficiency standards for vehicles."[3]

Matthew Goldberg is an associate research scientist at the Yale Program on Climate Change Communication at Yale University.[4] Matt's research focuses on persuasion, social influence, ideology, and strategic communication. He applies insights from the research to build public understanding and motivation to address climate change and other environmental, social, and political issues.

Matt recommends using simple, clear messages—and repeating them often. "That's probably the best rule of thumb," Matt says. "People need to know of the dangers, and they also need to know they're capable of meeting the challenges."

Matt's research also suggests that most people are open to discussions about climate change. "Sixty-six percent of

Americans say the issue of global warming is personally important, yet a similar proportion of Americans say they rarely or never talk about global warming with their friends and family. Many people mistakenly believe that other people don't care about global warming, which perpetuates the lack of discussion," he says.

His research also shows that most Americans already grasp the connection between renewable energy sources and a cleaner environment. "People's understanding of the role of renewable energy in reducing emissions varies widely, and that will depend a lot on your politics, where you live, and engagement with the issue," he says. "Even though many people do not totally understand the role of renewable energy in mitigating climate change, our surveys find that large majorities of Americans appreciate other benefits of renewable energy, such as cleaner air and water."

I find Matt's observations especially fascinating. Don't assume that someone you meet doesn't want to talk about energy and climate change—there's a good chance that you can get a conversation going and that you will find common ground.

From my perspective, a strong message always includes a call to action. A good message doesn't just scare people—it also empowers them and inspires them to retake control of their destiny. I find it useful to combine a clear description of the threat with a reminder that people and communities have the power to fight back.

How to Respond When Someone Says Climate Change "Is Natural"

Despite overwhelming scientific evidence, there are still plenty of people who don't want to believe that our energy habits are driving climate change. Here's one way to respond when someone tells you climate change isn't something to worry about because it's all part of a natural cycle:

Yes, climate change isn't a new phenomenon. Climate change can have many causes, including shifts in the earth's orbit, volcanic eruptions, and solar activity. The climate change we're experiencing now is different, and we can trace the causes to burning fuels such as coal, oil, and gas for energy. Thousands of scientific studies support the conclusion that the climate change we're experiencing today is due to human activities.

Focus on the Positives

The benefits of using energy more sensibly are extensively documented. The apocalyptic risks of ignoring our energy problems are also widely known, but harping on them excessively isn't going to win people to our side. Even people who believe in climate change and global warming need persuasion to change their behaviors.

For example, if all of our homes and buildings were better insulated, their carbon emissions would shrink and the positive impact on our environment would be significant. Insulation is a great way to fight climate change, and it's relatively easy. But homeowners and building owners are more likely to take action if you talk about the short-term economic benefits of well-insulated buildings, rather than focusing on the long-term risks of climate change.

Transportation is a major source of energy waste and pollution. When I talk to people about bicycle paths, hiking trails, and pedestrian-friendly neighborhoods, I highlight the health benefits of exercise, the opportunities to socialize, and the increased foot traffic to local stores.[5]

Frame the discussion to match the interests of your audience, and I guarantee they will respond more positively. "What do most people care about? They care about health, safety, and money," says Will Needham, founder of Future-Distributed.org, a knowledge-sharing platform focused on improving the built environment. "Instead of talking about reduced carbon emissions, talk about how your home or building will become cleaner, healthier, and more valuable after you've insulated it."

When you're talking to homeowners about solar energy, stick to the basic economics of solar panels and how easy it is to install them. If you're talking to politicians about wind turbines, keep the conversation focused on clean energy jobs and reduced government spending.

I can talk about increasing grid efficiency until the cows come home and nobody will listen. But when I talk about increasing building efficiency, I know building owners are listening because it will save them money and make their buildings more commercially attractive.

I like the idea of retrofitting and improving existing buildings for the simple reason that most of the world's buildings have already been built. Unquestionably, you can build a new building that's more energy efficient, more economical, more sustainable, and less destructive to the environment than an older building. But there will always be more older buildings than newer buildings, and these older buildings are enormous sources of pollution and waste.

That's why we need to focus on unsexy improvements such as thermal insulation, smart lighting, window blinds, and replacing old boilers. In the United States, residential and commercial buildings consume 76 percent of the nation's electricity and produce 40 percent of the carbon emissions.[6] Retrofitting older buildings is a responsible and uncontroversial strategy for reducing energy waste on a large scale.

Politicians Need Reminding

A disturbing trend I've noticed is the declining interest of politicians in energy issues. Many of the elected officials I know survey their constituents on a regular basis and post lists showing their top concerns. Energy and environmental issues are almost always on these lists, but they're rarely near the top.

That's a problem, because politicians tend to focus on the top three issues cited by their constituents. If energy and the environment aren't in the top three, they're probably not getting the attention they need and deserve.

I asked Matt how to convince greater numbers of elected officials to take climate change more seriously. Here's his response: "Make it an issue that people vote on. If elected officials don't see the issue of climate change as electorally consequential, then it's hard to move those officials in the right direction."

Today, many candidates for public office talk freely about promoting clean energy and reducing carbon emissions. If voters take these issues seriously, they will have to press candidates to develop well-conceived plans and hold them accountable for driving those plans to completion once they are elected. In other words, if we care about the environment, we can't just let the politicians talk—we need to make sure they follow through on their promises.

It's not all that difficult to persuade politicians to act on energy and environmental issues. But they need to know that voters actually care. In the movie *Jerry Maguire*, Cuba Gooding Jr. says, "Show me the money!" Politicians running for elected office say, "Show me the votes!"

In our complicated world, it's easy to forget the exquisitely simple relationship between politicians and voters. They need our votes to win elections. "Nothing motivates a politician more than the prospect of winning or losing an election," says Nathaniel Stinnett, founder and executive director of the Environmental Voter Project, a nonpartisan nonprofit using data analytics and behavioral science to identify and mobilize nonvoting environmentalists. "Politicians will always go where the votes are. That's the basic arithmetic of democracies."

Because energy is heavily regulated by government, politics plays an absolutely critical role in the development of energy policy. "Politicians have an enormous amount of control over where we go as a society with energy," Nathaniel says. "That's why electoral politics is so important. Politicians don't get to make policy unless they win elections."

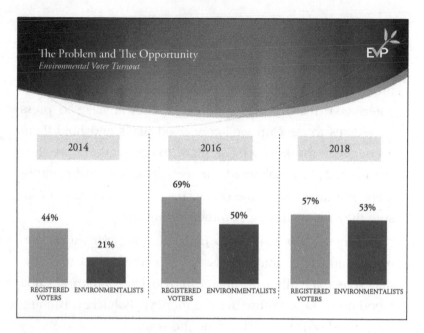

Figure 12.1 Environmentalist Voter Turnout
Source: Environmental Voter Project.

If you're wondering why more politicians haven't jumped on the clean energy bandwagon, the answer will come as an embarrassment: compared to other groups, environmentalists are inconsistent voters. In other words, they often fail to cast their votes on election day. From my perspective, that's inexcusable. Figure 12.1 illustrates the challenge. If everyone who says they're concerned about the environment voted, our politicians would respond.

Sharing Knowledge across State Lines

We live in a big country, with fifty states and thousands of communities. Maintaining the momentum of a national crusade is difficult, to say the least. The clean energy movement and related causes have spawned hundreds of organizations across the United States, and keeping them in sync has been an ongoing challenge.

One of the organizations I admire for its steadfast commitment to collaboration is the Clean Energy States Alliance (CESA). The group was formed in 2002, yet its roots stretch back to the deregulation of electric utilities in the late 1990s. Deregulation opened the door to greater competition, but many of the details were left to the states. As a result, each state developed its own unique approach to deregulation, relying on an array of policies and programs:[7]

- Renewable Portfolio Standards (RPS)
- Public benefit funds (PBF) for renewable energy
- Output-based environmental regulations
- Interconnection standards
- Net metering
- Feed-in tariffs
- Property assessed clean energy (PACE)
- Financial incentives

CESA grew from an effort to provide a collaborative learning network for states that wanted to promote clean energy and were coming to grips with the complexities of deregulation. Here's an excerpt from the CESA website:

> *Some states found a solution in mandating a small surcharge on ratepayers' electric bills—called a system benefit charge—that would go into a fund dedicated to developing clean energy resources. Managers of these new clean energy funds were left with the task of figuring out how best to use the money to advance renewable energy deployment in their state.*[8]

Warren Leon serves as CESA's executive director. In conversations, he invokes the idea popularized by US Supreme Court Justice Louis Brandeis that the states are "laboratories of democracy" in which new ideas are conceived and tested.

"A number of states had established clean energy funds to advance solar, wind, hydro, and other clean energy technologies," Warren explains. "Those states with the funds realized pretty quickly that it didn't make sense for them to operate in isolation, come up with programs independently, and not learn from each other. There was no point in reinventing the wheel each time a state wanted to develop a new program."

According to its website, "CESA works with state leaders, federal agencies, industry representatives, and other stakeholders to develop clean energy programs and inclusive renewable energy markets."[9]

CESA activities include the following:

- **Information exchange and analysis.** CESA supports a growing peer network of states interested in learning from each other and joining forces to expand the markets for clean energy technologies. CESA publishes several newsletters, hosts frequent webinars, and provides other opportunities for shared learning.

- **Partnership development.** CESA jumpstarts new strategic partnerships among the states, the federal government, and private sector players to accelerate clean energy investment.

- **Joint projects.** CESA works with groups of states to tackle major challenges and to achieve their clean energy goals.

- **Client services.** CESA delivers quality technical assistance and expertise on clean energy to its members, working with the national energy labs to provide analysis of renewable energy technologies and markets. CESA also represents the interests of state clean energy programs in national forums.[10]

"By all working together on the same issue at the same time, the states make greater progress than they would if they were just operating independently," Warren says. In addition to exchanging information, "they're providing moral support for each other." CESA engenders the collaborative spirit and enthusiasm necessary for completing long-term projects. When CESA members in one state see their work adopted or advanced by groups in another state, "they feel good. It validates that they were on the right track," says Warren.

The focus on collaboration also tends to overshadow the partisan bickering that often accompanies public projects. "Despite severe partisanship at the national level, blue states and red states are interested in exchanging information on clean energy, sharing ideas, and working together," Warren says. "We recently launched the 100% Clean Energy Collaborative[11] for states that have adopted goals and are getting 100 percent of their electricity from clean energy. That's all very encouraging."

Internal Business Communications

How you communicate about energy within an organization will be a major factor in determining the success of your energy projects. A good internal communications program will achieve several objectives:

- Motivating, informing, and educating colleagues about the specific tasks required to save energy and use energy more economically
- Reinforcing the idea that energy projects benefit the organization, its employees, the surrounding community, and the environment
- Setting the bar and establishing internal standards for more conscientious use of energy within the organization
- Clarifying decision-making processes for energy projects and programs
- Changing habits and long-term behaviors at the individual and group levels by sharing success stories and creating clear reasons for using energy more efficiently and effectively
- Promoting a spirit of collaboration and collegiality for energy programs
- Inspiring buy-in, participation, and engagement in energy programs over the long term

Always remember that a good communications strategy will have a direct influence on the success or failure of your internal energy programs. In fact, your communications strategy will be the heart of the process—the actual steps are relatively easy, but you'll need to convince people first that their efforts will bear fruit. The initial and most critical step is explaining the program and showing people how it will benefit them and benefit the organization.

Don't be shy about establishing guidelines, principles, and policies. People need more than ideals and platitudes—it's okay to set rules and hold people accountable for making sure the rules are followed.

Layers of Communications

Each project and program will be different and will involve different sets of individuals within the organization. Some initiatives will span the organization, and some will be limited to specific departments or operational areas.

Here's an example:

- The board creates a capital project agenda for the following year that includes the replacement of a boiler.
- The board communicates with the facility manager their desire to replace the boiler.
- The facility manager communicates with the energy-efficiency fund who issues incentive money to verify current equipment in the facility and communicates what type of new product will qualify for incentives satisfying the pre-inspection needed.
- The facility manager sources a new boiler and presents the proposal to the purchasing manager.
- The purchasing manager orders the boiler and then files for the incentive or rebate money.
- The purchasing manager notifies the CFO or controller that the new boiler qualifies for a tax deduction as a 179D energy-efficiency measure.

- The CFO or controller notifies the company's tax advisor.

- When the project is complete, the facility manager notifies the energy-efficiency fund to return to the location to review that the boiler installation is in accord with what was stated to be put in and additionally satisfying the post-inspection requirement.

This will complete the process necessary to receive the incentive money and the potential tax deduction. With little variation this process applies to power generation projects as well. In a renewable generation project, there may be a tax credit instead of a tax deduction.

Visual Cues and Rewards

Awareness creates action. Studies show that in the work environment visual awareness creates behavior change. A monitor with an energy dashboard displaying the consumption or creation of energy correlates with energy-efficient behavior. When energy is kept at the forefront of the mind of employees, employees respond by acting more energy efficiently.

An energy management system or building management system will provide a dashboard that can be placed in the front entrance, the cafeteria, or other general meeting space in the company for all to see.

Posters, emails, web pages, and energy-themed company events are excellent techniques for reminding people about the importance of internal programs and keeping them engaged. Rewards, gifts, and citations recognizing good energy practices are also great incentives.

The long-term goal is changing habits and influencing behaviors that will result in measurable savings and improved use of energy. You can't change the way people think and behave overnight—it's a process and there are no shortcuts.

Endnotes

1. https://flowcharts.llnl.gov/content/assets/images/energy/us /Energy_US_2019.png
2. https://climatecommunication.yale.edu/publications/climate -change-harms-human-health/
3. https://www.pewresearch.org/science/2020/06/23/two-thirds -of-americans-think-government-should-do-more-on-climate/
4. https://climatecommunication.yale.edu/
5. https://climatehealthconnect.org/wp-content/uploads/2018/10 /Guide_Section5.pdf
6. https://www.energy.gov/sites/prod/files/2017/03/f34/qtr -2015-chapter5.pdf
7. https://www.epa.gov/statelocalenergy/state-renewable-energy -resources
8. https://www.cesa.org/cesa-history/
9. https://www.cesa.org/about-cesa/
10. Ibid.
11. https://www.cesa.org/projects/100-clean-energy-collaborative/

Appendix A

Tips for Saving Energy at Home

Here are sixteen excellent tips for saving energy when you're doing laundry, written by Allison Casey of the National Renewable Energy Laboratory[1] and quoted verbatim from the DOE website:[2]

1. **Wash with cold water.** Using warm water instead of hot can cut a load's energy use in half, and using cold water will save even more. Cold water detergents can be helpful to ensure items get clean, and high-efficiency detergents (indicated by the "he" symbol) should be used when required by the manufacturer.

2. **Wash full loads.** Your washer will use about the same amount of energy no matter the size of the load, so fill it up.

3. **Dry right-sized loads for your machine.** If the dryer is too full, it will take longer for the clothes to dry. Loads

that are too small can also take longer to dry, plus you spend more per item when running the dryer to only dry a few things.

4. **Air dry when you can.** Hang laundry outside or on a drying rack to avoid using the dryer altogether.

5. **Switch loads while the dryer is warm.** This will allow you to use the remaining heat inside of the dryer for the next cycle.

6. **Use dryer balls.** Wool or rubber dryer balls will help separate your clothes and get more air to them, cutting drying time. They can also reduce static so you don't need dryer sheets (see #7 below). The wool balls are said to absorb some moisture, further cutting drying time. We use these at my house and have seen a noticeable difference in the time it takes our clothes to dry.

7. **Clean the lint filter on the dryer.** The dryer will run more efficiently and safely. If you use dryer sheets, scrub the filter once a month with a toothbrush to remove film buildup that can reduce air circulation.

8. **Use the high-speed or extended spin cycle in the washer.** This will remove as much moisture as possible before drying, reducing your drying time and the wear on your clothes from the high heat of the dryer.

9. **Use lower heat settings in the dryer.** Even if the drying cycle is longer, you'll use less energy and be less likely to over-dry your clothes.

10. **Dry towels and heavier cottons separately from lighter-weight clothes.** You'll spend less time drying the lighter-weight clothes.

11. **Use a cool-down cycle if your dryer has one.** This cycle allows clothes to finish drying with the heat remaining in the dryer.

12. **Use the moisture sensor option if your dryer has one.** Many new clothes dryers come designed with a moisture sensor, which automatically shuts off the machine when clothes are dry. This will save energy and reduce wear and tear on your clothes caused by over-drying.

13. **Sign up for time-of-day programs with your utility.** These programs offer lower energy costs at certain times of day—often overnight. If you can plan to do your laundry overnight (or use controls on your machine to schedule washing or drying), you can pay less to do your laundry. Contact your utility for more information.

14. **Use an ENERGY STAR–certified washer and dryer.** New ENERGY STAR washers use about 25% less energy than conventional models, and ENERGY STAR dryers use 20% less energy.

15. **Consider a gas dryer.** Depending on gas and electric rates in your area, a gas dryer could cost less to operate, though it may cost a little more to purchase. Keep in mind a gas dryer does need a dedicated gas line.

16. **Consider a heat pump dryer.** The initial cost may be a bit higher, but heat pump dryers can save 20%–60% over conventional dryers by taking in ambient air, heating it, and recirculating it. There are some things to consider if you decide to buy a heat pump dryer—namely sealing old dryer vents and drainage. Visit ENERGY STAR for more information.

The changing seasons also provide opportunities for reducing power use and saving money. Here's a handy list of energy-saving steps to take in the springtime,[3] compiled by Paul Lester of the DOE:

- **Service your air conditioner.** Easy maintenance such as routinely replacing or cleaning air filters can lower your cooling system's energy consumption by up to 15%. Also, the first day of spring could serve as a reminder to check your air conditioner's evaporator coil, which should be cleaned annually to ensure the system is performing at optimal levels.

- **Open windows.** Opening windows creates a cross-wise breeze, allowing you to naturally cool your home without switching on air conditioners. This is an ideal tactic in spring when temperatures are mild.

- **Use ceiling fans.** Cooling your home with ceiling fans will allow you to raise your thermostat four degrees. This can help lower your electricity bills without sacrificing overall comfort.

- **Cook outside.** On warmer spring days, keep the heat out of your home by using an outdoor grill instead of indoor ovens.

- **Install window treatments.** Energy-efficient window treatments or coverings such as blinds, shades, and films can slash heat gain when temperatures rise. These devices not only improve the look of your home but also reduce energy costs.

- **Caulk air leaks.** Using low-cost caulk to seal cracks and openings in your home keeps warm air out—and cash in your wallet.

- **Bring in sunlight.** During daylight hours, switch off artificial lights and use windows and skylights to brighten your home.
- **Set the thermostat.** On warm days, setting a programmable thermostat to a higher setting when you are not at home can help reduce your energy costs by approximately 10%.
- **Seal ducts.** Air loss through ducts can lead to high electricity costs, accounting for nearly 30% of a cooling system's energy consumption. Sealing and insulating ducts can go a long way toward lowering your electricity bills.
- **Switch on bathroom fans.** Bathroom fans suck out heat and humidity from your home, improving comfort.

Endnotes

1. https://www.nrel.gov/
2. https://www.energy.gov/energysaver/articles/16-ways-save-money-laundry-room
3. https://www.energy.gov/articles/10-energy-saving-tips-spring

Appendix B

Resources

For more information on tax credits:

http://energy.gov/savings/business-energy-investment
-tax-credit-itc

http://energy.gov/savings/qualifying-advanced-energy
-manufacturing-investment-tax-credit

For more information on depreciation and tax deductions:

https://www.irs.gov/publications/p946/ch04.html

http://www.energy.gov/savings/modified-accelerated
-cost-recovery-system-macrs-bonus-depreciation
-2008-2012

https://www.irs.gov/irb/2008-14_IRB/ar12.html

http://www.dsireusa.org

For more information on tax exemptions:

CT: http://www.ct.gov/drs/lib/drs/forms/2005forms/certificates
/cert-115.pdf

NY: http://www.tax.ny.gov/pdf/publications/sales/pub852
.pdf

MA: http://www.mass.gov/dor/docs/dor/forms/wage-rpt/pdfs
/st-12.pdf

http://www.mass.gov/dor/docs/dor/forms/wage-rpt
/pdfs/st-13.pdf

For more details:

http://www.dsireusa.org

For more information on your state's Public Benefit Fund
options:

http://www.c2es.org/us-states-regions

For more information on PACE financing:

http://pacenow.org/resources/all-programs/

For the federal government and its incentive programs:

http://energy.gov/eere/about-us/office-energy-efficiency
-and-renewable-energy-contacts

http://www.worldpopulationbalance.org/population
_energy

https://www.energystar.gov/buildings/about-us
/facts-and-stats

BIBLIOGRAPHY AND RECOMMENDED READING

Bakke, Gretchen. *The Grid: The Fraying Wires between Americans and Our Energy Future*. New York: Bloomsbury USA, 2017.

Barlow, Mike, and Cornelia Lévy-Bencheton. *Smart Cities, Smart Future: Showcasing Tomorrow*. Hoboken, NJ: Wiley, 2018.

Barnes, Peter. *With Liberty and Dividends for All: How to Save Our Middle Class When Jobs Don't Pay Enough*. San Francisco: Berrett-Koehler, 2014.

Barnes, Peter. *Who Owns the Sky? Our Common Assets and the Future of Capitalism*. Washington, DC: Island Press, 2001.

Beavan, Colin. *No Impact Man: The Adventures of a Guilty Liberal Who Attempts to Save the Planet, and the Discoveries He Makes about Himself and Our Way of Life in the Process*. New York: Farrar, Straus and Giroux, 2009.

Boyce, James K. *The Case for Carbon Dividends*. Medford, MA: Polity Press, 2019.

Caro, Robert A. *The Years of Lyndon Johnson: The Path to Power*. New York: Vintage Books/Random House, 1981.

Emanuel, Kerry. *What We Know about Climate Change*. Cambridge, MA: The MIT Press, 2018.

Esty, Daniel C., and Andrew S. Winston. *Green to Gold: How Smart Companies Use Environmental Strategies to Innovate, Create Value, and Build Competitive Advantage*. Hoboken, NJ: Wiley, 2009.

Fridley, David, and Richard Heinberg. *Our Renewable Future: Laying the Path for One Hundred Percent Clean Energy*. Washington, DC: Island Press, 2016.

Jonnes, Jill. *Empires of Light: Edison, Tesla, Westinghouse, and the Race to Electrify the World*. New York: Random House Trade Paperbacks, 2004.

Meadows, Donella H. *Thinking in Systems: A Primer*. White River Junction, VT: Chelsea Green Publishing, 2008.

Pollin, Robert. *Greening the Global Economy*. Cambridge, MA: The MIT Press, 2015.

Raworth, Kate. *Doughnut Economics: 7 Ways to Think Like a 21st Century Economist*. White River Junction, VT: Chelsea Green Publishing, 2017.

Schendler, Auden. *Getting Green Done: Hard Truths from the Front Lines of the Sustainability Revolution*. New York: PublicAffairs, 2009.

Seaton, Hugh. *The Construction Technology Handbook: Making Sense of Artificial Intelligence and Beyond*. Hoboken, NJ: Wiley, 2021.

Smil, Vaclav. *Energy and Civilization: A History*. Cambridge, MA: The MIT Press, 2018.

EXPERT SOURCES

Peter Asmus is research director for microgrids at Guidehouse Insights, focusing on emerging energy distribution, integration, and optimization platforms such as microgrids and virtual power plants and distributed energy resource management systems. He has thirty years of experience in energy and environmental markets as an analyst, writer, and consultant. His expertise also extends to renewables such as wind power, solar energy, hydrokinetics, and advanced energy storage technologies.

Peter has been managing Guidehouse Insight's microgrid syndicated research service since 2009. In that role, he has served as the lead author of more than seventy-five different reports covering topics as diverse as different microgrid global market segments (ranging from off-grid, remote communities to direct current [DC] data centers), capacity and revenue forecasts, technology evaluations, and regulatory analysis. During the course of this research, he has also profiled more than one hundred market players active in this microgrid space.

He is the author of four books covering key energy market issues: *Reaping the Wind, Introduction to Energy in California, Reinventing Electric Utilities*, and *In Search of Environmental Excellence*. He is a frequent speaker at industry conferences and he is quoted regularly in major publications including the *New York Times,* the *Washington Post, The Christian Science Monitor,* and Reuters.

Brandon Barnes is a senior energy analyst for Bloomberg Intelligence, a unique research platform that provides context on industries, companies, litigation, and government policy. He has been covering the energy sector for Bloomberg since 2014, specializing in the analysis of litigation, regulation, and liability affecting energy companies and the broader industry. He is the team leader for the energy team, which includes equity, litigation, and policy analysts covering a number of sectors.

He earned a bachelor of arts from the University of North Carolina at Chapel Hill as well as a JD from Wake Forest University School of Law. He has been admitted to practice law in Maryland, District of Columbia, several federal courts, and the US Supreme Court.

Ed Boman is assistant director of public works and energy manager for the Town of Fairfield, Connecticut. His duties have included negotiating a $7 million energy performance contract; the development of thirty-five municipal solar facilities and a fuel cell; the installation of two microgrids, one for public safety and the other for public health; and negotiations for a new virtual net metering facility and a community solar facility. He graduated from the University of Bridgeport with a master's degree in political science.

James K. Boyce is an author, economist, and senior fellow at the Political Economy Research Institute at the University of Massachusetts Amherst. He holds a doctorate from Oxford University. His most recent books are *The Case for Carbon Dividends* (Polity, 2019) and *Economics for People and the Planet:*

Inequality in the Era of Climate Change (Anthem, 2019). He has written for *Harper's, Scientific American,* the *New York Times,* the *Los Angeles Times,* and numerous academic journals including *Proceedings of the National Academy of Sciences, Ecological Economics, Climatic Change,* and *Energy Policy.* He is the recipient of the 2017 Leontief Prize for Advancing the Frontiers of Economic Thought.

Kim Cheslak is an associate director for New Buildings Institute (NBI). She supports NBI's national engagement in code and policy development, with an emphasis on national model codes, stretch codes, and building performance standards. She has more than ten years of experience focusing on buildings and codes. Prior to joining NBI, she worked for the Institute of Market Transformation, leading commercial and residential code compliance studies, and working with local governments to maximize savings through adoption of and compliance with energy codes.

She has a master of architecture, master of urban design, and master of social work from Washington University in St. Louis, as well as a bachelor of science in architecture from the University of Maryland.

Angus Duncan is the founding president of the Bonneville Environmental Foundation, which supports renewable energy development and watershed restoration in the Pacific Northwest. He has worked in private sector renewable energy project development, in state and local government, as a member and chair of the Northwest Power Planning Council, and as director of energy policy, US Department of Transportation. In 2004 he chaired the Drafting Committee that wrote Oregon's greenhouse gas reduction goals and climate strategy, since adopted by the governor and legislature. He served as chair of Oregon's Global Warming Commission 2008–2020. He consults with NRDC on energy and climate policies in the Pacific Northwest.

Matthew Goldberg is an associate research scientist at the Yale Program on Climate Change Communication at Yale University. His research focuses on persuasion, social influence, ideology, and strategic communication. He applies insights from his research to build public understanding and motivation to address climate change and other urgent environmental, social, and political issues. Matthew holds a BA in psychology from Hofstra University and received his PhD in psychology from the Basic and Applied Social Psychology program at The Graduate Center, City University of New York.

Rob Kaye is the cofounder and president of Nod Hill Brewery in Ridgefield, Connecticut. He is also the owner and operator of Riverside Fence, a provider of quality custom fencing.

A serial entrepreneur, he has owned and operated several successful businesses, including a company that managed sports merchandise concessions for the US Tennis Open, the NCAA Final Four, the 1996 Olympics, and various minor league baseball teams. He also operated the Meadowlands Flea Market in New Jersey for fifteen years.

Rob is a graduate of Bryant College (now Bryant University) in Smithfield, Rhode Island.

Tim Kelley has twenty-five years of power industry experience, including utility-scale and distributed power generation development, power trading and risk management, independent system operator transaction software systems, energy management, and demand response, smart grid, distributed generation, and renewable and microgrid technology. He has held leadership positions in finance and development at Green Mountain Power; Lodestar Software (now part of Oracle's Energy Suite of products); Weidmann Electric Technology; American Capital Energy, a developer of commercial and utility scale solar projects; and Russelectric. He was a founding member of Green Mountain Energy, the country's first marketer of renewable power in unregulated energy markets. His focus is driving opportunities at the intersection of sustainable technology, energy markets, and capital.

He has a BS in computational mathematics from the University of Vermont and an MBA from Rensselaer Polytechnic Institute.

Warren Leon is executive director of the Clean Energy States Alliance (CESA). He oversees the organization's day-to-day operations and leads strategy development. He has written and edited many reports for CESA, including serving as lead author for *Returning Champions: State Clean Energy Leadership since 2015* and *Solar with Justice: Strategies for Powering Up Under-Resourced Communities and Growing an Inclusive Solar Market.* Prior to working for CESA, he was director of the Massachusetts Renewable Energy Trust, executive director of the Northeast Sustainable Energy Association, and deputy director for programs at the Union of Concerned Scientists. He coauthored the influential book *The Consumer's Guide to Effective Environmental Choices.* He holds a PhD from Harvard University.

Jason F. McLennan is considered one of the world's most influential individuals in the field of architecture and green building movement today. He is a globally, highly sought out designer, consultant, and thought leader. He is the recipient of the prestigious Buckminster Fuller Prize (the planet's top prize for socially responsible design). He has been called the Steve Jobs of the green building industry and a "World Changer" by *GreenBiz* magazine. Jason is the creator of the *Living Building Challenge*—the most stringent and progressive green building program in existence—as well as a primary author of the *WELL Building Standard*.

He is the founder of the International Living Future Institute and is the CEO of McLennan Design—his own architectural and planning practice designing some of the world's most advanced green buildings. His work has been published in dozens of journals, magazines, and newspapers around the world.

Will Needham is the creator of FutureDistributed.org, the global knowledge-sharing platform that aims to transition the built environment sector so that it supports thriving citizens and a thriving planet. Future Distributed produces data-informed, interactive, and inspiring content to help built environment professionals take positive action. He initially trained in architectural engineering (Loughborough University, UK) before completing a master's degree in data science (City, University of London, UK). He is a professionally accredited chartered construction manager with the Chartered Institute of Building.

Nick Nigro is the founder of Atlas Public Policy. He has more than fifteen years of experience managing projects of various disciplines, size, and scope. He is a nationally known expert on alternative fuel vehicle financing, policy, and technology. He has led the development of several complex financial and policy analysis tools, convened large groups of diverse stakeholders nationwide, managed a comprehensive analysis of greenhouse gas mitigation from US transportation, is a frequent public speaker on advanced vehicle technology and other transportation-related energy and environmental issues, and has expert knowledge in web and other computer-related technology. He holds a master of public policy from the University of California Berkeley's Goldman School of Public Policy and a bachelor of science in electrical and computer engineering from Worcester Polytechnic Institute.

Dr. Sandeep Nimmagadda is director of the Global Laboratory Energy Asset Management & Manufacturing (GLEAMM) project at Texas Tech University in Lubbock, Texas. As director, he manages TTU's GLEAMM microgrid facility built for research, testing, and certifying innovations using wind, solar, battery storage, weather forecasting, PMU, cybersecurity, and control systems design located at Reese Technology Center.

His previous work with Apex Clean Energy and GE has afforded him the experience in implementing complicated solutions in power plants to improve performance of operating assets, instilling a passion for tech start-ups, renewable energy, microgrids, electric vehicles, water conservation, and waste management.

Bernie Pelletier has had an interest in energy independence and renewables since the Arab Oil Embargo in the 1970s. When he retired from his position as a property casualty actuary in Hartford, he devoted himself to working for a sustainable future. He is the chair of the West Hartford Clean Energy Commission and serves as vice president for PACE. Most recently he is acting chairman of the GC3's Building Mitigation Working Group.

In his professional career, he worked on a large variety of risk problems in the United States and internationally. Now he uses the quantitative analytics of the actuarial profession and brings them to bear on the technical and social challenges that stand between today's unsustainable world and a future world that is sustainable, in all the senses of that word, and resilient in the face of the inevitable political and climate disruption now facing us.

Mark Scully is president of the nonprofit People's Action for Clean Energy and is actively engaged in promoting Connecticut's transition to clean, renewable energy. He retired in 2017 from a thirty-five-year career as an actuary and from 2018 to 2020 oversaw the restoration of a local historic mansion, the Ensign House in Simsbury, Connecticut, into a mixed-use commercial property, using modern, energy-efficient technology and practices. Over his career, he served as chief actuary of several international insurance companies, including Allianz Group, AIG, and Ironshore Inc. Prior to these roles, he was a principal at Willis Towers Watson and the founder of that company's property-casualty consulting practice in Germany.

He received his BA in mathematics and German from Washington and Lee University and his MA in international economics and foreign policy at the Paul Nitze School of Advanced International Studies of Johns Hopkins University. He is a fellow of the Casualty Actuarial Society and a certified passive house consultant.

Hugh Seaton has a lifelong passion for technology and has worked in marketing, product development, and general management for international companies such as Sony Electronics, Google, Philips Electronics, and more. He is the author of *The Construction Technology Handbook* (Wiley, 2021), which reflects his decade of work in the broader built environment. He frequently consults on IoT, VR/AR, and other emerging technologies.

He has a joint MBA from Columbia University and London Business School and spent ten years of his career in international postings, primarily greater China, where he is fluent in Mandarin.

Nathaniel Stinnett is the founder and executive director of the Environmental Voter Project, a nonpartisan nonprofit using data analytics and behavioral science to identify and mobilize nonvoting environmentalists. Hailed as a "visionary" by the *New York Times* and dubbed "the Voting Guru" by Grist, he has over a decade of experience as a senior advisor, campaign manager, and trainer for US Senate, Congressional, and mayoral campaigns as well as issue-advocacy nonprofits. Formerly an attorney at the international law firm of DLA Piper LLP, he holds a BA from Yale University and a JD from Boston College Law School.

Amy Thompson joined the University of Connecticut in August 2017 as an associate professor-in-residence of systems engineering and as the associate director of academic programs with the United Technologies Corporation Institute of Advanced Systems Engineering (UTC-IASE). She currently teaches model-based systems engineering and coordinates the online graduate programs in advanced systems engineering for the UTC-IASE.

Prior to joining UConn, she received her BS in industrial engineering, MS in manufacturing engineering, and PhD in industrial and systems from the University of Rhode Island and she taught systems engineering to undergraduate and graduate students for six years at the University of New Haven. She also worked with an interdisciplinary team to create a BS and BA in sustainability studies at the University of New Haven and taught courses in design for environment and sustainability.

Scott Thompson is the volunteer chairman of the Sustainable Fairfield Task Force where he lives in Fairfield, Connecticut. As a volunteer, he has led the development of Fairfield's Clean Energy Action Plan (2014) and Sustainability Plan (2018). Through the task force's efforts, the town has developed more than six megawatts of local clean energy generation, two microgrids, and implemented several award-winning sustainability initiatives. Through the task force's advocacy, more than five hundred Fairfield residents installed solar energy systems at their homes. Scott is also one of Connecticut's leading advocates for electric vehicle (EV) adoption, lecturing on EV adoption throughout the northeastern US.

He is a licensed professional engineer and a certified sustainability professional with more than twenty-five years of experience. He is an international consultant who manages technically advanced environmental engineering and utility scale renewable energy projects and he has made his professional career as an engineer and vice president of WSP USA. As a project or program manager, he has delivered more than $90 million of professional services for public- and private-sector clients, meeting or exceeding profit goals. Daily, he assists municipalities, universities, and companies to identify and achieve sustainability goals, with a focus on renewable energy projects and EV infrastructure. To date, he has led the development and design of eight hundred MW of commercial solar and wind energy projects.

Chris Ulbrich earned his bachelor's degree in labor management and finance from the University of Connecticut. After graduating from college, he accepted a position at Ulbrich Stainless Steels and Special Metals Inc. as a director of purchasing. In 1988, he was promoted to executive vice president and remained in his position of director of purchasing and sales. During this time, he was responsible for operations supporting 225 employees worldwide and all global sales and activities. In 1993, he became the president of Ulbrich Service Centers. From 1995 to 2014, he was COO of Ulbrich. As COO, he provided pivotal leadership in building new operations and internal acquisitions. In 2014 he was appointed chairman and CEO after the passing of the second generation, Frederick C. Ulbrich Jr. Although the company continues to grow in size, services, and revenue, he strives to maintain the highest quality services and leadership. During the most turbulent times in the twentieth century, he provided strength and support to Ulbrich employees and their customers. Ulbrich has grown to 690 employees in twelve locations on three continents.

Since 1991, he has served on the board of directors to the Young Presidents Organization and organizer of Castle Bank in Meriden, Connecticut. In 2006 to current day, he has been involved in Central Connecticut's Community Foundation. In addition, he has been an advocate in promoting wellness within the company as well as in the community. He was also a member on Mid-State Medical Center's Community Board and provided board support to the United Way; YMCA in Wallingford, CT; and other Connecticut businesses and industries since 2010. He is active in the Boys & Girls Club in Wallingford, Connecticut.

Christopher Vigilante is the chief operating officer of Northside Development Company, where he leads the day-to-day financial management of the company. He is also involved in the development process from planning, financial forecasting, government approvals, and construction forecasting. He has been with Northside Development Company for fifteen years and in the real estate industry for eighteen years. He has been involved with developing in excess of $65 million worth of real estate. His awards and recognition include the Congressional Recognition Certificate presented by Connecticut Representative Rosa DeLauro, Alderman Certificate for Community Service, and Award for Outstanding Contribution presented by the New Haven Police Department. He has been a member of the Board of Zoning Appeals for five years.

He also participates in charitable organizations including Habitat for Humanity, March of Dimes, American Red Cross, Yale New Haven Children's Hospital, and the New Haven Christmas Run.

Elisa Wood is a cofounder of RealEnergyWriters.com. She leads a team of versatile energy writers that produce copy for some of the top energy companies, trade associations, and organizations. She has been writing about energy for more than two decades and has contributed widely to McGraw-Hill/Platts, Pennwell, and other energy industry publishers. Her blogs have been picked up by CNN, the *New York Times* blog-runner, the *Wall Street Journal* Online, *USA Today*, Reuters, *Mother Earth News*, Real Clear Energy, the *Washington Post*, and others. She is also the author of many reports, guides, white papers, and web content that look deeply at energy issues in an engaging, accessible writing style. These include the frequently downloaded Think Microgrid series, published by Microgrid Knowledge, where she serves as editor-in-chief.

Before beginning her freelance career, she served as publications director for Emerson College in Boston and worked as a staff writer for daily newspapers in Colorado and Massachusetts. She has won awards from the New England Press Association, the Iowa Press Association, the National Council for the Advancement and Support of Education, and others.

ABOUT THE AUTHOR

Elena Cahill is an attorney, educator, business executive, investor, and entrepreneur. She is a respected thought leader and energy industry consultant with decades of hands-on experience.

She serves as director of the Ernest C. Trefz School of Business College of Engineering, Business, and Education at the University of Bridgeport, a post she has held since 2018. Previously, she was a senior lecturer at the University of Bridgeport, specializing in law and entrepreneurship. She holds a BS and JD (Juris Doctor) in finance and law and is the founder of the University of Bridgeport Student Entrepreneur Center.

Elena Cahill is a warm and engaging speaker, with a wealth of stories and real-world experiences that she shares with her audiences. When practicing law as a partner at Tyler Cooper and Alcorn, she worked with large energy clients such as Iberdrola and Southern Connecticut Gas Company, which led to her interest in energy management and strategy.

In 2009, she founded Globelé Energy, LLC, a women-owned professional energy service firm located in New Haven, Connecticut. Globelé Energy benefits the commercial and industrial sector by providing customized solutions for energy conservation, efficiency and generation services, outsourced energy management and auditing services, and energy procurement services for both electricity and natural gas.

She was also the CEO and founder of Aequitas Energy, Inc., a deregulated electric supply company licensed in Connecticut and Massachusetts. Her daily responsibilities included financing and hedging energy products, regulatory matters, developing customer interface, and hiring the management and sales team. Aequitas was sold to a private investment firm in July 2014.

Elena Cahill is a current member of the Association of Energy Engineers, the Town of Branford Ad Hoc Energy Committee, CTNext Higher Education Innovation Advisory Board member, and a board member of the Entrepreneur Foundation and the Connecticut Consortium of Entrepreneur Educators. She is a prior board member of the Connecticut Power and Energy Society.

INDEX

layers of, 169–170
networks,
    high-speed, 34
politicians
    and, 162–164
positives, focus
    on, 160–162
simple, clear
    messages, 158
strategy for, 168–169
visual cues, rewards
    an, 170–171
Completed projects,
    savings and, 153–155
Connecticut, 24, 74–78,
    115–116, 117, 124,
    132, 135, 140,
    142, 145, 149
Connecticut
    Green Bank, 64
Conservation. *See*
    Energy conservation
*The Construction Tech-
    nology Handbook*
    (Seaton), 7
Contracts, 131, 132, 133
Costs. *See also* Energy
    bills; Pricing energy
    electricity, 110–112
    energy efficiency
    and, 8

municipality and, 77
"trophy" building
    energy pro-
    ject, 71, 72
wind and solar energy
    systems, 33, 77–78
C-PACE programs, 151
Culture, 18, 30–31, 35,
    44, 47, 157–158

D
Data. gov website, 111
DC (direct current)
    motors, 9–10
Decarbonization,
    EVs and, 36
Demand rate, elec-
    tricity, 122
Demand response pro-
    gram, 147–148
Demand stabiliza-
    tion, 15–27
batteries and, 32
demand load
    and, 123–124
energy ecosystem
    and, 25–27
islands of energy, 19–21
microgrids and, 21–25
techniques and strate-
    gies for, 18–19

Incentives, energy-
efficient prac-
tices and, 170
Infrastructure, 11,
112, 113, 118,
121, 134, 148
Insulation, building,
101, 160–161
Interest-rate buy-downs,
149–153
Internal combustion
engines, 36
International Energy
Conservation Code
(IECC), 94
Islands of energy, 19–21

J
Johnson, Lyndon, 35

K
Kelley, Tim, 22, 24–25
Kilo volt ampere reac-
tive (KVAR), 10–11
Knowledge shar-
ing, 164–167

L
Law/legal
framework for, 84–89
Northwest Power
Act, 88–89

universal property
and, 46–48
LED lighting, 13, 55, 68,
70, 71, 146
Leon, Warren, 166, 167
Letter of agreement
(LOA), 143, 144
Lighting/light bulbs. *See
also* LED lighting
energy conservation
and, 98–99
motion sensors on, 59
older-style, 12
retrofitting of,
101, 103, 118
Lithium-ion batteries, 30
Living Building
Challenge, 2–3
Living buildings, 2–4
Loans, 149–153
Local action, 73
PACE and, 78–84
public works depart-
ment and, 74–78
Local tax exemptions,
141–142

M
Machine learning, 34
Market economics, 51
Market shocks, 118